Melania
& Michelle

Melania
& FIRST LADIES IN A NEW ERA
Michelle

Tammy R. Vigil

RED ⚡ LIGHTNING BOOKS

This book is a publication of

Red Lightning Books
1320 East 10th Street
Bloomington, Indiana 47405 USA

redlightningbooks.com

Manufactured in the United States of America

Library of Congress Cataloging-in-Publication Data

Names: Vigil, Tammy, author.
Title: Melania and Michelle : first ladies in a new era / Tammy R. Vigil.
Description: Bloomington, Indiana : Red Lightning Books, [2019] |
    Includes bibliographical references and index.
Identifiers: LCCN 2019011000 (print) | LCCN 2019019640 (ebook) |
    ISBN 9781684350988 (ebook) | ISBN 9781684351015 (hardback : alk.
    paper) | ISBN 9781684350995 (pbk. : alk. paper)
Subjects: LCSH: Presidents' spouses—United States—Biography. |
    Presidents' spouses—United States—History—21st century—
    Case studies. | Presidents' spouses—Political activity—United States
    —History—21st century—Case studies. | Trump, Melania, 1970- |
    Obama, Michelle, 1964-
Classification: LCC E176.2 (ebook) | LCC E176.2 .V54 2019 (print) |
    DDC 973.09/9 [B] —dc23
LC record available at https://lccn.loc.gov/2019011000

1 2 3 4 5 24 23 22 21 20 19

For

ANDREW

The third time is still charming.

Contents

Illustrations follow page 65.

Acknowledgments

FIRST, I AM GRATEFUL TO ASHLEY RUNYON, ACQUISITIONS EDITOR at Indiana University Press, for inviting me to consider this topic. She initially prompted me to examine the first ladyships of Michelle Obama and Melania Trump, which led me to unearth both some surprising similarities as well as some telling differences between the women. The project also created a space for interrogating the difficulties presidential spouses confront throughout their time in the public eye. It was a fruitful experience, and I owe Ashley many thanks for the challenge.

I am also indebted to Andrew L. Crick, friend and life partner. As a wordsmith and grammarian, and as a sounding board and source of support, I rely on him heavily and he never lets me down. Without his diligence, persistence, and encouragement, I could not do what I do. Writing can be a lonely enterprise, and I appreciate the spirit of camaraderie Andrew brings to my various research endeavors.

Finally, this book would not exist without the women who have served the country as first lady of the United States. Enduring constant scrutiny from numerous quarters regarding everything from their person to their politics, these women have nevertheless persevered in their efforts to fulfill the often unclear, frequently unrealistic, and sometimes even contradictory expectations we, the public, place upon them. Pat Nixon famously said, "Being first lady is the hardest unpaid job in the world," and, after writing this book, I am inclined to agree.

Melania & Michelle

Introduction

Comparing First Ladies

IT IS NEITHER SURPRISING NOR UNUSUAL FOR INDIVIDUALS TO want to compare the women who have served as first lady of the United States. Even the first ladies have measured themselves against their predecessors, beginning when Abigail Adams expressed concern about how she would meet the standards set by Martha Washington. Since the nation's founding, the press and the public have taken a keen interest in presidents' mates and have interpreted, evaluated, and critiqued the women most intimately connected to the purported leader of the free world both individually and relative to one another. Discussions about each new first lady regularly include queries about her potential changes to the White House and her approach to the role as a national public figure. As each presidential administration changes, the nation becomes fascinated with the alterations in décor and decorum the new matron of the White House might bring.

All first ladies eventually forge their own unique path in what is an uncertain role, but only a handful of first ladies become memorable figures who are frequently used as points of comparison for those who follow. These women distinguish themselves by embracing or fighting social norms, by creating impactful public agendas, or by building unique and enduring public images. Eleanor Roosevelt became an idealized model of the active first lady by being what many considered an unconventional spouse in a time when women's political empowerment was increasing, whereas Jacqueline "Jackie" Kennedy became a fashion icon whose quietude and focus on motherhood earned her much praise. These particular women cast long shadows among their peers and are the two first ladies most frequently used in assessments of contemporary presidential mates, but they are certainly not the only ones. Claudia "Lady Bird" Johnson, Rosalynn Carter, and Barbara Bush are often used as exemplars of first lady activism for their efforts promoting highway beautification, mental health, and literacy, while Thelma "Pat" Nixon constructed an endearing public persona as an "all-American" first lady due to her down-to-earth style and folksiness.

Not all presidential spouses have been used as positive benchmarks. Nancy Reagan was chided for her expensive tastes and her tendency to insert herself into critical staffing decisions in the West Wing. Although her husband was beloved by many, Nancy Reagan was heavily criticized and developed into the antitheses of the Jackie Kennedy prototype. In the 1990s, Hillary Clinton emerged as a negative counterpoint to so-called traditional first ladies. Her more masculine clothing style (including structured pantsuits with padded shoulders), claims of being an intellectual and professional equal to her husband, and willingness to engage in policy discussions were considered hallmarks of assertiveness that many people felt made her unladylike. During the 2000 campaign and most election cycles of the twenty-first century, wives of presidential candidates have tried in both conspicuous and subtle ways to establish themselves as the "anti-Hillary," and political pundits have continually made overt comparisons between would-be first ladies and Mrs. Clinton. Even decades after she left the White House, politicos still implied and sometimes stated outright that political spouses closer in character to Clinton were less fit to oversee the East Wing than those who adopted more conventional perspectives.

Whether positive or negative, assessments of new first ladies routinely begin with references to the women who previously filled the role. Unfortunately, such appraisals tend to rely heavily on selective characterizations of past White House matrons that present them in narrow ways by highlighting one or two cherry-picked attributes rather than considering the more complex nature of their lives, perspectives, and actions.

The practice of trying to understand the women who hold the most potentially influential unelected political position in the United States continues here with an examination of the two most recent modern first ladies, Michelle Obama and Melania Trump, and the formation of their public personas. To provide commensurate insights regarding Obama and Trump, the two are discussed within the various contexts of their time in the spotlight as political spouses, including during the presidential campaign, their transition to the White House, and their first ladyship. Additionally, how each forged her own path as first lady, the various criticisms and controversies that both first ladies managed, and their negotiation of the role during their spouses' reelection bids all receive particular attention. In each case, historical anecdotes about their predecessors demonstrate the wide range of approaches used by those who previously undertook the duties of a presidential consort. The stories also provide context for considering the impact of the past on these contemporary women.

In November 2016, when Donald Trump won the presidency and Melania Trump was slated to replace Michelle Obama as the first lady of the United States, mainstream and social media reporters began to actively contrast the two women. The ladies were generally cast as extremely different people with little in common. Michelle Obama was portrayed as an Ivy League–educated woman from a lower-middle-class family who worked hard to overcome race- and gender-based challenges. Melania Trump was depicted as an uneducated foreigner with not much to offer beyond her physical looks. Obama appeared as a coequal partner with her spouse and as someone who made personal sacrifices in order to assist her husband in his patriotic endeavors, whereas Trump seemed like a trophy wife who enjoyed the benefits of having married a wealthy older man. The initial comparisons were clearly more favorable toward Obama and critical of Trump. However, such side-by-side analyses were fundamentally unfair because Obama enjoyed the benefits of her incumbency while Trump was new to the position and, in spite of her minor celebrity status, was not very well known. By 2016, the press and public were quite familiar with Obama because she had spent almost ten years on the national stage (as a presidential contender's spouse and as first lady), yet they knew Trump mostly as a former model who was married to a reality television star. A closer look at these women's lives indicates that, while the two were unique individuals who had different experiences, attitudes, and personalities, they also had more similarities than their public personas seemed to indicate.

Michelle Obama, like many other accomplished wives of presidential nominees, suspended her professional career to support her husband's White House bid. At the time of Barack's formal announcement, Michelle had taken a leave of absence from her lucrative position with the University of Chicago Hospitals. Having earned a bachelor's in sociology (with a minor in African American studies) from Princeton in 1985 and a degree from Harvard Law School in 1988, Obama was an Ivy League–educated attorney who left the legal profession after a few short years at a prestigious Chicago law firm in order to pursue more public-service-oriented ventures. She worked as the assistant to the mayor of Chicago, developed community outreach and volunteer programs, and eventually secured a position at the University of Chicago. In less than a decade, she rose from associate dean of student services, to executive director of community relations and external affairs for the medical center, and then to vice president of community and external affairs for the university's hospitals.

In a number of interviews, Michelle Obama credited her professional successes to her personal support system. Born Michelle LaVaughn Robinson on January 17, 1964, the self-styled "girl from the south side" of Chicago had a financially modest but emotionally stable childhood; she was raised in a conventional nuclear family consisting of her parents and one brother. She was surrounded by extended family, including the aunt whose home the Robinson clan lived in and other relatives in the neighborhood. In the early 1990s, she met and eventually married Barack Obama. The couple had two daughters: Malia was born in 1998 and Sasha in 2001. Michelle Obama balanced the duties of wife, mother, and university executive with assistance from the many family members (several of whom babysat on occasion) who lived nearby. She often served as the family's primary breadwinner and buttressed her husband's burgeoning political career. When Barack set his political sights on the Oval Office, Michelle chose to shift her focus away from her own career development and dedicate more time to helping her husband meet his goals.

Melania Trump was born on April 26, 1970, in Novo Mesto, a city in what was then the state of Slovenia in Yugoslavia. Before becoming the first lady of the United States, Trump was best known as the third wife of celebrity businessman and reality television star Donald Trump. However, she had an interesting and varied life of her own prior to her marriage. Born Melanija Knavs, the eventual Mrs. Trump was raised, along with her sister, in austere housing. The family enjoyed an economically humble, but nonetheless secure, lifestyle due to her father's position in the local Communist Party. A pretty girl from her youth, Melania began modeling at a young age and was starring in television ads by the time she was sixteen years old. At eighteen, she signed with a professional modeling agency in Milan. She briefly attended college, but she opted to become a full-time model rather than complete her degree.

Trump's work in the fashion industry presented many opportunities. She modified her name to Melania Knauss in order to secure more jobs while she negotiated the competitive markets of Europe. In 1996, she relocated to the United States to further her career and accepted several lower-level modeling engagements despite lacking a proper work visa. Two years after establishing herself in New York, Melania met Donald Trump. Her association with the businessman increased her visibility, and, as a result, she soon began gracing the covers of prestigious magazines. Seven years later, Melania and Donald married. In 2006, Melania Trump gave birth to Barron (the couple's only child together) and officially became a US citizen. She stopped modeling to focus on motherhood but retained some business investments and became involved in philanthropic work. Although she was married to a noted publicity seeker, Trump's life took a largely private turn between the time her son was born and when her husband decided to run for president.

This thumbnail sketch of the women's lives before entering the national political spotlight offers points of comparison between the two and with their predecessors in the White House. Obama's and Trump's histories before they became potential first ladies (their time as presidential contenders' wives and as White House matriarchs are discussed in various chapters of this book) help demonstrate how the frames used to depict the women dictate how members of the press and the public perceive them because these first ladies can be affiliated with very different past presidential consorts depending on the focal points employed. For example, when commentators emphasize fashion and poise, both Michelle Obama and Melania Trump are regularly equated with Jackie Kennedy. However, this particular connection is just one narrow way of viewing these women. Most other topics routinely used to evaluate the spouses of US presidents yield different pairings.

Since women began earning undergraduate and advanced degrees in larger numbers, the level of education attained by presidents' wives has been a frequent point of assessment. In 2008, Michelle Obama became just the fourth first lady to have earned a graduate degree, aligning her with Pat Nixon, Hillary Clinton, and Laura Bush. Obama and Clinton are the only two who earned juris doctor degrees, and they each did so from elite law schools (Harvard and Yale, respectively). Near the other end of the educational spectrum, Melania Trump's academic experience makes her similar to Rosalynn Carter and Barbara Bush; all three women started college but never completed a degree. For Trump and Carter, their formal schooling ended because of occupational and financial pressures; Bush quit school to get married and start a family.

Professional accomplishments provide a slightly different lens for interpreting the relationships between first ladies. In this regard, Michelle Obama arguably most resembles Hillary Clinton in that each woman earned a spot at a prestigious law firm (Obama in Chicago, Clinton in Arkansas) and had a higher salary than her husband throughout much of her prepresidential life. Trump's career progression was more akin to that of Betty Ford and Nancy Reagan. These three women worked in competitive image-oriented industries (Trump as a model, Ford as a dancer, and Reagan as an actress). Additionally, as a young woman, Ford was a fashion model for a local department store, but her efforts did not expand into a career like Trump's did. The occupational paths of both Obama and Trump reflect a competitive spirit and drive to build an impressive portfolio. Such characteristics are identical to those displayed by Lady Bird Johnson (a self-made millionaire who established her own modest media empire) and Hillary Clinton.

Some perhaps unexpected associations among first ladies emerge when considering what are often deemed more traditional aspects of these women's lives, like their relationships with their children and husbands. Almost all presidents' wives had children (though not necessarily with the spouse who won the Oval Office), but their number of offspring ranged from the eight kids Leticia Tyler and Lucy Hayes each bore to the zero children from Sarah Polk (the only childless first lady). Obama, like Johnson, Nixon, and Laura Bush, had two daughters and no sons. Trump, like Hillary Clinton, gave birth to only one child. Obama, Trump, and Clinton all waited until well into their thirties to have children and all three were raising school-aged kids (as was Rosalynn Carter) when they assumed the mantle of first lady. Obama and Trump shared the experience of motherhood in an additional way; neither woman hired a nanny to assist in the raising of her children. Obama relied heavily on family members to help her balance between her parental duties and her professional responsibilities. Trump quit her modeling career to focus on motherhood. As a working mom Obama was similar to Clinton, and as a stay-at-home mother Trump was akin to Laura Bush.

Even though it is not possible to fully understand the nature of a couple's private relationship from the outside looking in, based on external appearances Michelle Obama and Melania Trump seemed to have very different kinds of marriages. The Obamas were only ever married to each other. They were comparable in age (Barack was three years older than Michelle), and stories about them gave the impression that they had a loving connection and a partnership that blended customary and modern divisions of labor; Michelle was frequently the parent most responsible for the children's care, but she at times was also the family's main source of economic support. One anecdote about Obama taking her youngest daughter with her on a job interview when she could not find a babysitter illustrates how she fulfilled both conventional and unconventional roles, caring for her daughter and expanding her career. Much like Lady Bird Johnson and Hillary Clinton, Obama was a working mother who created financial security for the family while undergirding her husband's political ambitions. Other presidents' spouses who were employed outside the home until their husbands ran for office include Pat Nixon (who was a teacher, a secretary, and an economic analyst), Rosalynn Carter (who ran the family's peanut farm), and Nancy Reagan (who continued acting until she became the first lady of California in the mid-1960s).

The Trumps' pre–White House relationship was different from the Obamas' in many ways. Melania, twenty years younger than her husband, was Donald's third wife. The age difference, coupled with his presumed wealth and reputation for being unfaithful, caused many people to question the nature of their marriage. Reporters habitually framed their union in more mercenary terms than those of most past presidential couples; Melania was portrayed as having married for money and security, while Donald was viewed as essentially buying a trophy wife in order to bolster his perceived virility.[1] While the validity of this perspective is debatable, the lack of public displays of affection between Melania and Donald, his occasionally crass public discussions about their relationship, and Melania's tendency not to speak publicly about her marriage encouraged negative speculation about their union. In many ways, the description of their marital bond as business-like recalled depictions of the Clintons' relationship throughout the 1990s and 2000s. Additionally, the fact that Melania quit her chosen profession after marrying Donald and focused on the activities of motherhood after the birth of Barron aligned her with a host of previous first ladies who had done the same. Betty Ford worked during her first marriage (to William Warren) and after her divorce, but she quit her employment outside of the home when she married Gerald Ford. Barbara Bush declared herself a career wife and mother. Laura Bush ceased her employment as a teacher and librarian upon marrying George W. Bush.

Although Michelle Obama and Melania Trump are often portrayed as having little in common, a review of their pre–White House lives shows that they had a variety of similar experiences and a series of comparable attitudes. For instance, both women were raised in less comfortable environments than their forerunners. Unlike most other modern first ladies, Obama and Trump grew up in economically and politically difficult situations. Nancy Reagan had a tumultuous early life, but it stabilized when she was nine years old and her mother married a wealthy and prominent neurosurgeon. Barbara Bush lived through the Great Depression, yet her family was able to employ house staff to help care for her and her siblings throughout the economic collapse. Laura Bush's father was a successful real estate developer, and Hillary Clinton was raised in a moderately affluent suburb of Chicago. In contrast, Obama and Trump each grew up in meager dwellings; Obama's family lived in a small apartment on the second floor of her aunt's home on the south side of Chicago, while Trump lived in a bland apartment building said to overlook factories with smoking chimneys.[2] Obama's neighborhood, while not the most dangerous in the city, was not the safe and relatively tranquil milieu of Midland, Texas (Laura Bush's hometown). Trump's youth was spent in a politically tumultuous region of Europe where she witnessed her country transform from a socialist state within federal Yugoslavia to an independent nation.

Both Michelle Obama and Melania Trump, as young girls, sought opportunities to improve their lives. Starting at a young age, Obama became an exemplary student and Trump became a model. Obama made sacrifices, like riding a bus for three hours a day to attend an elite charter school, in order to improve her future prospects in life. She also moved far from her home and close-knit family to attend Princeton University and Harvard Law School. Trump, likewise, made sacrifices to enhance her life. She changed her name to broaden her modeling prospects, dropped out of college to pursue professional opportunities, and eventually left her family and country with the hope of building an international career. While other first ladies also left their homes in pursuit of a better life, few made such big changes in their locations and circumstances as Obama and Trump did.

Michelle Obama and Melania Trump were both ambitious women, albeit in different ways. Obama pursued an advanced education and earned prestigious positions in both the private and public sectors. Melania Trump cultivated a career in an extremely competitive field and broke immigration laws in order to advance her vocational standing. Both women established their professional credentials before getting married, had children while in their thirties, and supported their husbands' pursuits. The eventual first ladies have quite a bit more in common than most people assume because the differences between Michelle Obama and Melania Trump are usually accentuated in public discussions about them.

Even though exploring the similarities between these first ladies is illuminating, it is important to remember that each woman was a unique individual with her own experiences, attitudes, and concerns. Michelle Obama was the first black woman to preside over the East Wing of the White House. She had to navigate a different set of social challenges while becoming and being the first lady than any of her predecessors. She was also arguably the most educated presidential spouse based on her multiple Ivy League degrees. Furthermore, Obama overcame many socioeconomic challenges throughout her life that other first ladies never faced. Melania Trump was just the second first lady not born in the United States—and the only one who was a naturalized US citizen. She was also the only presidential consort to have been raised in a communist country. Trump was considered the most linguistically skilled White House matriarch, claiming fluency in five languages, but her heavy accent and difficulty with American idioms created challenges for her that past first ladies did not endure. Trump was also a businesswoman with her own lines of jewelry and skin care products.

Looking at the handful of examples provided above, it is apparent that the links between first ladies of the past and present depend heavily on the characteristics under consideration. While both Obama and Trump are most frequently associated with Kennedy, they could just as easily be affiliated with Johnson, Reagan, and either Barbara or Laura Bush. Obama is akin to Nixon in many interesting ways, and Trump has much in common with Ford. Based on their lives before becoming presidential spouses, multiple metrics also align both women with Clinton. Although Obama, Trump, and Clinton are routinely cast as dissimilar women, the facts of their lives demonstrate otherwise. The reason, beyond simple partisan posturing, that these ladies are often considered antitheses of one another is because public perceptions of them are generally based on oversimplified caricatures rather than nuanced understandings. Because marital associations dominate popular interpretations of these influential individuals, first ladies are customarily portrayed much like underdeveloped members of a supporting cast—certain attributes and experiences are strategically highlighted, and few attempts are made to understand their full personhood. Still, the women who have served as first lady of the United States have been rather complex and interesting women with rich histories of their own.

Although the public personas of Michelle Obama and Melania Trump built by the press and by the women themselves usually frame the two as polar opposites, with Obama appearing more assertive and outgoing and Trump seeming quiet and aloof, the women are not entirely dissimilar. They share qualities such as a willingness to subordinate their needs in support of their husbands' agendas and a devotion to their children. To understand why their similarities are routinely overlooked and what they and others gain from their divergent portrayals, it is necessary to examine the formation and fortification of Obama's and Trump's outward identities throughout their time in the public eye. The ultimate goal is to explain how and why these women are viewed so differently and to discuss the ways in which directly contrasting the first ladies is unfair to both women. Public actions by the women offer insight into their decision-making regarding their image formation, and press coverage of the two illustrates how the various frames used to interpret the women shape public perceptions of them.

The first ladyship is a challenging position for any person to assume. It is a role that receives a great deal of attention, whether wanted or not, and carries a lot of potential, if unsanctioned, power. Yet, as an unelected office, the post is an ambiguous one that lacks a clear mandate and whose occupant must adapt to constantly changing social expectations and restrictions. With no clear job description to guide them, first ladies rely heavily on their communicative skills to maneuver through public life as the president's mate, whether through speeches, the development of social initiatives, the use of social media, their wardrobe choices, and even the strategic decision to be silent. Because any woman who takes up the first lady mantle is heavily scrutinized and routinely measured against idealized and hyperbolized memories of past first ladies, every action she takes opens the president's mate to critique. This has been particularly true for Michelle Obama and Melania Trump, as each tried to negotiate the important, but amorphous, political and social responsibilities shouldered by the first lady of the United States.

ONE

Auditioning for First Lady

Their Debut Presidential Campaigns

BEFORE EITHER MICHELLE OBAMA OR MELANIA TRUMP BECAME first lady of the United States, each had to endure the vetting process known as the presidential campaign. All modern would-be first ladies are now expected to participate in their husbands' election efforts. Even though the spouses do so in a variety of ways, the reasons for their involvement are largely the same. These individuals speak on behalf of their mates and provide additional insights into the character of the candidates. Also, despite the fact that they are not on the ballot, consorts gain considerable status, influence, and access to power if their mate wins the presidency, so the press and the public seek out information about potential first ladies' pasts, attitudes, and plans if they occupy the White House. The first lady possesses no codified governmental authority, but citizens still want to know what kind of national matriarch a candidate's spouse will be. In addition to the official electoral contest, the modern presidential campaign serves as an opportunity for candidates' spouses to audition for the position of helpmate to the president, a role that "continues to stand as a symbol of American womanhood."[1]

Although contemporary candidates' consorts face arguably more pressure to be publicly engaged figures than most wives of candidates historically did, every potential first lady throughout American history has forged her own path relative to campaigning. In the 1800s, women like Dolley Madison and Louisa Adams hosted social events intended to build political alliances that would aid their husbands' efforts to win the presidency. As time passed, women's activities expanded. In the latter half of the nineteenth century, Mary Baird Bryan helped create campaign strategies and wrote speeches that led her husband, William Jennings Bryan, to win the Democratic Party's presidential nomination three times. Throughout the twentieth century, as women became more politically empowered and new communication technologies made the dissemination of information easier, candidates' spouses became increasingly visible parts of campaigns. They gave radio interviews, appeared on television, and were featured in magazine and newspaper stories. Campaign strategies were built around popular spouses, and slogans like "I like Mamie, too" (an allusion to the "I like Ike" tagline in support of Dwight D. Eisenhower), "Pat [Nixon] for First Lady," and "Betty [Ford]'s Husband for President" emerged. Some mates were more active than others during the primaries and general elections, but many of the women married to presidential contenders started headlining fund-raisers and holding campaign rallies on their own.

By the mid-1990s, the spouses of presidential nominees had become featured surrogate electioneers and regular speakers at each major party's nominating convention. The presidential contests in the twenty-first century have seen spouses reach out directly to potential voters through traditional means and social media outlets. For all eventual first ladies, their spouses' initial campaigns were when the women established the public personas that influenced how they would be interpreted throughout their time in the White House. This held true for both Michelle Obama and Melania Trump.

GEARING UP FOR THE RACE

Almost two years before Barack Obama won the US presidency, Michelle Obama suspended her lucrative professional activities in preparation for her husband's campaign. She was initially ambivalent about Barack running for the highest elected office in America but was assured that the effort would not be a waste of time after she reviewed the detailed campaign plan she'd demanded potential staffers produce. Even while harboring concerns about the disruption the contest would cause for their family and worrying about the dangers running posed because of potential racial tensions that could arise, Michelle Obama supported her husband's decision to run and agreed to be an active participant in the campaign. She, along with the couple's two daughters, stood dutifully behind her husband as he formally announced his candidacy in Springfield, Illinois, on February 10, 2007. Even before that moment, though, Mrs. Obama had already become a national figure.

Michelle Obama first drew widespread notice at the 2004 Democratic National Convention (DNC) after her husband gave a stirring keynote address that is often credited with launching him onto the national political stage. Barack garnered most of the attention that night, but some members of the press were careful to mention the well-coiffed, stylishly dressed, and supportive spouse waiting for him backstage. Pictures of Michelle and Barack at the podium after his oration dominated newspapers and websites in the hours and days following the speech. Stories quickly emerged about the couple, and many cast Michelle Obama as an exemplary helpmate. The reports explained how she'd attended practice sessions where Barack learned to use a teleprompter, provided feedback on the content and delivery of the address, and made wardrobe suggestions the night of the event. One article claimed that Barack insisted his wife stay with him backstage rather than sitting in the audience because she gave him a sense of stability and calm that no one else could.[2] Many of the key positive features of Michelle Obama's eventually well-cultivated public persona—namely that she was active, bright, helpful, fashion-savvy, and supportive—were evident in several 2004 DNC anecdotes about her.

In 2008, many critics debated whether the Obamas were too new to national politics to really contend for the White House. Eight years later, a true political novice and his spouse sought to replace the Obamas. Because reality television star and known publicity seeker Donald Trump had previously teased the press with hints he might run for the presidency, his formal announcement on June 16, 2015, was initially treated as a hoax. Politicos around the nation wondered if the speech was simply some ploy to promote a new TV show, and most commentators thought he had no chance of winning the Republican nomination, much less the Oval Office. Few people took Donald Trump seriously in the early days of his campaign, and even fewer considered the possibility of Melania Trump as a potential first lady. So, unlike Michelle Obama, who endured at least four years of speculation regarding her role in a potential presidential bid, until a few months into the GOP primaries Melania Trump was treated only as the celebrity she'd become since she started dating Donald in the late 1990s. It was not until March 2016 that the media spotlight focused more directly on her.

For both Michelle Obama and Melania Trump, the respective primary contests that served as their first entrée into the national political realm were challenging. Each woman quickly learned that while she could influence the interpretive frames the public used to evaluate her, she was not the only one constructing such lenses. The press, the public, and the opposition also had a say in the public personas each developed.

THE PRIMARIES

The first nationwide contests Michelle Obama and Melania Trump participated in were their husbands' battles to earn a major party's presidential nomination. The primaries in 2008 and 2016 were interesting for a number of reasons. In both cases, there was no incumbent seeking reelection, so the preliminary races were truly party-centric contests. That meant the initial evaluations of both women happened as party members vied for the nomination. For the Democrats in 2008, eight serious contenders began the primaries, but by the end of January the battle focused on Illinois senator Barack Obama and former first lady (and New York senator) Hillary Clinton. The quick narrowing of the field meant that the spouses of both candidates received more extensive attention earlier in the process than did many past potential presidential helpmates. In 2016, seventeen Republicans declared their intent to become the GOP standard-bearer. Eleven made it to the primaries, four won party-based elections or caucuses, and three continued to compete well into May. Although in any other year the abundance of candidates might have led the press to concentrate on the candidates rather than their spouses, the Republican race turned its focus on the frontrunners' wives for a short time in mid-March when attacks were launched against Melania Trump and Heidi Cruz.

Another reason the 2008 and 2016 primaries were intriguing was because of the distinctive nature of the candidates and their spouses. The 2008 Democratic contest quickly became historic when it was clear that for the first time either an African American or a woman would win a major party's nomination. The competitors' mates were a well-educated black woman and a former US president with a scandalous past. Because they were both unique candidate spouses, Michelle Obama and Bill Clinton received a great deal of consideration by the media as politicos contemplated the ways each might behave as a presidential consort. The struggle for the GOP nomination in 2016 also comprised a wide array of people. The field was made up of white, black, and Latino men and one affluent white woman. Their spouses were equally diverse and included one man and two immigrants who'd become naturalized US citizens.

The historical context and tenor of a presidential race sometimes dictates how and when the spouses become focal points in national contests, but so do the personalities of the mates and their willingness to engage with the public. In 1992, for example, Hillary Clinton drew a great deal of attention from the press very early in her husband's presidential bid. Her assertion that she was a coequal partner in her marriage and her willingness to publicly spar with reporters and with her husband's opponents meant Clinton was thrust (and also propelled herself) onto center stage of the presidential campaign shortly after the primaries began in earnest. For Michelle Obama, her decision to speak on behalf of her husband meant she became an early surrogate campaigner, drawing regard and scrutiny soon after the 2008 Democratic contest started. Melania Trump maintained a much more retiring demeanor, giving no speeches and few interviews, yet the hostile tone of the 2016 primaries essentially forced her into the campaign when GOP candidates began attacking one another's spouses. Even though Michelle Obama and Melania Trump entered the limelight at different times and in different ways, both had to maneuver through life as prominent public figures while their husbands pursued the presidency.

When the race for the White House officially commenced for the Obamas, the press seemed inclined to positively interpret the potential first lady. Described as blending "the poise of Jackie Kennedy with the brain of Hillary Clinton and the uncomplicated charm of Laura Bush,"[3]

Obama was often touted as a caring wife and capable partner. Discussions about her life routinely centered on the fact that she and her husband had comparable degrees and similarly humble beginnings. These shared experiences purportedly gave the couple a unique understanding of one another and created a sincere bond between them. Stories about their union also tended to reinforce the supposed normalcy of their relationship by casting Michelle Obama as a modern version of a customary wife. She was talked about as the more practical part of the pair, the one in charge of the day-to-day running of the household, and the one who assumed most of the child-rearing responsibilities. She also was said to be responsible for converting her husband's idealistic thinking into feasible action. Journalists proffered an image of Obama as an intelligent working mother whose first duty was to her family.

During the early days of the 2016 campaign, the media painted a less complimentary picture of the Trumps and particularly of Melania. News stories about the couple emphasized the fact that Melania was Donald's third wife and twenty years his junior. Tales about Donald's past infidelities called into question the nature of the couple's union and invited readers to view Melania as motivated by the accumulation of wealth and status rather than by a sincere love for her husband. Her usual silence at campaign rallies and the limited number of interviews she gave during the primary campaign led commentators to doubt whether Trump truly supported her husband's candidacy. With no stories about Melania serving as a private adviser or even a confidant to her husband, the Trump marriage appeared to be not a partnership but a somewhat mercenary arrangement with a very traditional orientation (a male provider dominating over an ostensibly submissive female).

Although they were portrayed in very different ways during the early days of their initial national campaigns, one aspect of Melania Trump's public image that aligned with Michelle Obama's was that she was a caring mother. Throughout their respective campaigns, the sincerity of both women's devotion to their children was never questioned. Obama was touted as a loving and concerned working mom who arranged her campaign commitments in a way that regularly allowed her to be home with her daughters. Trump, likewise, was depicted as a committed mother who refused to hire a nanny because she viewed motherhood as her most important responsibility in life. While many aspects of both women's character regularly came under fire during their husbands' initial bids for the White House, their dedication to motherhood was not one of them.

Michelle Obama and Melania Trump each continued a long tradition among eventual first ladies by both willingly and begrudgingly becoming visible parts of their husbands' campaigns. The differences in their participation reflect the range of approaches political wives have taken in fulfilling their roles as helpmates. Obama embraced her position as a campaign surrogate and behaved in a similar fashion to many contemporary candidates' spouses. She was active in strategic planning efforts and was a vocal part of planned events. Obama demanded a clear delineation of the campaign staff's strategic vision and pushed for the preparation of contingency plans throughout the contest. She also gave speeches at rallies she headlined, hosted high-dollar fund-raisers, and gave many media interviews. She appeared alone almost as often as she did with her husband. Obama blended the strategic savvy of Barbara Bush (deemed the "Silver Fox" for her cunning behind-the-scenes contributions) with the forthright nature of Hillary Clinton and the convivial personality of Pat Nixon.

Melania Trump developed a more subdued approach to campaigning that encouraged some pundits to liken her to Jacqueline Kennedy and to Laura Bush during the 2000 campaign (Bush became much more vocal and active in 2004). Trump was fairly reticent, gave few interviews, rarely attended events without her husband, and avoided expressing her opinions on political topics. Comparing Trump to Kennedy made sense because both women seemed to have a distaste for politics and shared an interest in fashion. Each of these women gave the impression of being aloof and indifferent when it came to campaign strategy. Both also pointed to their maternal duties in order to avoid campaigning. Trump's connection to Bush, however, depended on a limited understanding of Laura Bush's political acuity. During the 2000 campaign, Bush offered a counterpoint to the assertive sitting first lady, Hillary Clinton, by claiming to be a reluctant campaigner. Seemingly reserved and submissive, Bush was actually a more seasoned political operative than many members of her husband's staff; she'd spent more than twenty-five years assisting with electoral contests at the state and national level. Whether her purported shyness was genuine or a strategic effort to win over voters with anti-Hillary sentiments, Bush's relative silence on the campaign trail was nowhere near that of Melania Trump's in 2016. In fact, Trump's outward manner during the 2016 GOP primaries was among the least expressive of all modern eventual first ladies. Even the very traditional Mamie Eisenhower came across as a more enthusiastic part of her husband's national campaign than Melania Trump did.

The primary contests in 2008 and 2016 provided early lessons regarding the expectations the future first ladies would face and the constraints sociohistorical contexts would place on Michelle Obama and Melania Trump once they moved into the East Wing of the White House. The manufactured controversies each woman withstood during the spring of her husband's campaign highlighted the ways the press and the opposition influenced perceptions of the women and underscored the conventional preferences the public had for the behavior of presidential spouses. In Obama's case, her words were used against her, and for Trump, her past came back to haunt her.

In mid-February 2008, at a campaign rally in Madison, Wisconsin, Michelle Obama made a comment that would dog her for the duration of the campaign and much of her time in the White House. Talking about the nation's expressed desire for change, Obama conveyed her regard for voters in a way that many critics argued illustrated her lack of national loyalty and framed her as an ungrateful person. The line "For the first time in my adult life, I am really proud of my country"[4] drew condemnation because it appeared unpatriotic and, as one news correspondent contended, "reveal[ed] an edge of bitterness Michelle Obama felt."[5] The press regularly replayed the abbreviated clip of her statement, usually without an explanation of the context in which she said it. Obama's remark became grounds for attack from both Democratic and Republican opponents of her husband. The words also encouraged detractors to examine Obama's history. They dissected essays she had written about racial tensions in America when she was an undergraduate student at Princeton and presented excerpts from her writings as though they were recent comments. This tactic was reminiscent of one employed against Hillary Clinton in 1992 when research she'd conducted about parent-child relationships several decades earlier became the basis of negative depictions of her. In both cases, the old papers were used to paint the women as extremists—Obama as anti-American and Clinton as anti-family. In 2008, for voters who were disinclined to support an African American woman as matriarch of the White House, the sound bite and old documents became evidence of Obama's unfitness to be the first lady.

Trump's troubles with the press began in mid-March 2016 when the GOP primaries took a very personal and heated turn. Donald Trump had volleyed many personal attacks at his opponents even before the contest had begun, but many of his comments were dismissed as inconsequential rants from someone who would soon be out of the race. However, by March it became clear to many contenders that Donald was a genuine threat requiring a response. Some candidates and commentators then tried to use negative tactics against the emerging frontrunner by making derogatory remarks about the businessman-turned-showman-turned-politician, but they didn't always stop with statements about Donald. In early March, a series of images and memes began circulating through social media. The photographs, originally taken by *GQ* magazine fifteen years before the election, showed a nude Melania laying across a fur blanket. They were combined with text questioning the potential first lady's morality. One set of such memes endorsed Ted Cruz. The Cruz campaign denied any responsibility for the leaked photos, but Donald Trump retaliated by threatening to share secrets about Cruz's wife and others. The mudslinging and salacious content of the photos drew widespread attention. The mainstream news picked up the story and published the pictures across various media.

The effort to discredit Donald Trump by claiming Melania was unfit to be the first lady hearkened back to negative campaign strategies of the past. Political operatives once spread rumors about Dolley Madison having had an affair with Thomas Jefferson in order to dissuade voters from supporting James Madison for president. Newspaper editorials pressed voters to shun Andrew Jackson because his wife, Rachel, known for riding horseback with a western saddle and occasionally smoking a pipe, was not ladylike enough to be the White House matron. Eleanor Roosevelt's alleged lesbianism and friendships with African Americans were viewed as liabilities for her husband. Hillary Clinton was said to not only be unladylike herself but to despise anyone embracing traditional femininity. For Melania Trump, the nude photos that emerged in March 2016 were recycled throughout the primaries in different forms. A second set of pictures was published at the outset of the general election campaign.

The criticisms of Michelle Obama and Melania Trump spoke to long-held perspectives about the social and political role of modern candidate spouses. When Obama shared an opinion that ran even mildly contrary to the presumed norm, she was scorned. Similar to the infamous 1992 Hillary Clinton comment about not wanting to stay home and bake cookies, Obama's statement about being proud of her country was taken out of context and abbreviated to sound more disparaging than it actually was. Still, the response to Obama's words indicated that actual, if amorphous, boundaries existed regarding what was and was not acceptable behavior for a candidate's wife. The spouse of a potential president was expected to be deferential, traditional, and patriotic. The complaints about Trump were also grounded in assumptions that potential first ladies fulfill particular functions. In Trump's case, she was said to lack the ability to act as an effective moral guardian, a duty generally assigned to women (especially maternal figures). The possibility that she had acted in a less-than-respectable manner in her nude photo shoot led to questions about Trump's ability to serve as a role model of American womanhood, particularly for young girls.

Michelle Obama's early missteps presented lessons that helped shape the way she later managed her public persona. While she did not shy away from expressing herself, she did tend to couch many of her comments in terms that appeared more acceptable from the wife of a presidential contender. At campaign events, during press interviews, and on various television shows, she most frequently spoke about her role as a mother and a wife, framed her political interests in terms of a maternal perspective, and engaged in humorous exchanges that often included self-deprecating jokes intended to demonstrate her humility. Obama embraced this more customary perspective as a means of building connections between herself and the audience of potential voters she was trying to win over. This approach enabled Obama to transcend some perceived differences between herself and past first ladies, as well as between her and the public at large.

The mainstream press offered a generally approving image of Obama that affirmed her as an exemplar of conventional femininity by focusing on her actions as a wife and mother, her trendy fashion choices, and her healthy physique (particularly her envy-inspiring arms). Her intellectual ability was mentioned but rarely celebrated in its own right. Reporters occasionally wrote or spoke of Obama's Ivy League education but scarcely mentioned specific aspects of her professional work. Most stories about the eventual first lady highlighted her intelligence by describing her wittiness, particularly as it was directed toward her husband. Journalists underscored Obama's efforts to keep her husband grounded by repeatedly writing about her public complaints regarding his tendency to leave dirty socks outside the laundry basket, forget to put away the butter after making toast, and fail to make the bed.[6] When Obama reminded audience members that her husband was "a gifted man . . . but just a man,"[7] most reporters applauded her for making him seem relatable, but a few denounced her for being a disrespectful mate. As members of the media discussed how Obama humanized her husband, they also depicted her as an average woman who had the same kinds of experiences as many wives and mothers across America. Michelle Obama cultivated an "everymom" persona the press could easily digest and the public could relate to and sympathize with regardless of presumed racial and socioeconomic differences.

Melania Trump's negative insertion into the 2016 GOP primaries did not seem to spark much of a change in her activities or the messaging around her. Some politicos condemned the very existence of the lewd photos, while others berated whoever was responsible for leaking the fifteen-year-old pictures. Commentators lamented the alleged weaponization of spouses' pasts and framed Trump as a victim of dirty campaign tricks. Donald defended Melania by threating to expose secrets about the wife of a rival, yet little was heard directly from Melania Trump. She continued to periodically stand on stage with her husband and occasionally sit beside him during interviews, but she did not publicly defend herself, try to explain away the photos, or justify her actions.

By the end of their respective primary contests, Michelle Obama and Melania Trump had established themselves in the minds of many voters. Perhaps because of her more vocal and varied public pronouncements,

Obama was better known and better liked than Trump at similar points in their campaigns. Seventy-eight percent of voters had a clear opinion of Michelle Obama before the 2008 Democratic National Convention (DNC), and 60 percent had a definite view of Melania Trump ahead of the 2016 Republican National Convention (RNC).[8] What's more, 53 percent of respondents said they held a favorable opinion of Obama in 2008, whereas only 28 percent regarded Trump positively in 2016.[9] The difference between the percentage of people holding positive and negative perspectives on Trump at the end of the primaries placed her net favorability at minus 4 percent. This made Melania Trump the least-liked eventual first lady of the modern era based on preconvention polling.

Pinpointing the specific cause of the difference in public perceptions of Michelle Obama and Melania Trump before their husbands' nominating conventions is beyond the scope of this book, yet several distinctions between the women and their situations are evident. Michelle Obama was far more engaged in the campaign and made herself more accessible to the media in 2008 than Melania Trump did in 2016. Obama showed a great deal of personality and purposefully tried to connect with a variety of diverse citizens throughout the primaries; Trump did not speak often and rarely appeared alone, raising questions about her actual interest in the campaign and providing no personal anecdotes for audience members to identify with. In addition, Obama benefited from her husband's popularity, while Trump suffered from her association with a polarizing candidate. For Michelle Obama and Melania Trump, the pivot toward the general election offered an opportunity to reinforce or redefine her outward image as each woman addressed a national audience.

THE NATIONAL CONVENTIONS

Michelle Obama and Melania Trump both participated in their husbands' nominating conventions. The gatherings of delegates, leaders, and other interested individuals generally mark the turning point from the party-focused primary battles to the national campaign that pits established nominees directly against one another.[10] The meetings traditionally provide each party the opportunity to hold the media spotlight for several days and to formally present its presidential candidate to the nation. In addition, the events give the public a chance to meet other major characters in the election, including vice presidential nominees and potential first ladies.[11]

For much of American history, the spouses of nominees played a limited role in the conventions. In the mid-to-late 1800s, the wives of candidates were not present during the assemblies because the raucous affairs were considered no place for a lady. However, as processes for selecting nominees evolved, so did the form and function of the conventions, broadening the scope of attendees and speakers. In the early twentieth century, nominees' mates became fixtures at the conventions, and some were strategically deployed to help their husbands. First Lady Helen "Nellie" Taft attended both the RNC and DNC in 1912. Her presence at the DNC was intended to discourage speakers from aggressively criticizing her Republican husband, William Taft. In 1920, Florence Harding, wife of Warren G. Harding, gave interviews to the press in the hallways of the convention center and encouraged reporters to write about Warren's kindness and concern for children. Breaking with traditions of the time, in 1940 Eleanor Roosevelt became the first spouse of a nominee (and the first sitting first lady) to address a convention. She presented what some deemed a philosophical speech that advocated for her husband without using his name or referencing his office. It was the first and most idiosyncratic of all spouses' convention speeches. The feat would not be repeated until Barbara Bush took the stage at the RNC in 1992. In the intervening years, wives of party nominees continued to appear at conventions, usually standing beside their husbands while posing for photos and occasionally being honored on stage for their work as first lady.

Since Barbara Bush delivered a full, scripted speech at the 1992 RNC, it has become a tradition that nominees' spouses address party delegates and the nation at their respective conventions. It is the largest audience the consorts encounter during a campaign, and it is frequently touted as a consequential moment. When any mate of a major party's presidential nominee speaks from the convention stage, she or he faces an unusually daunting task because individuals in this situation are charged with meeting multiple goals. They try to establish their own connection to the audience; to demonstrate their ability to perform as a potential presidential helpmate; and to win support for the candidate by extolling the nominee's credentials, humanizing the potential president, and providing personal insights into the would-be commander in chief's character. The spouses of challengers for the White House (as opposed to an incumbent running for reelection, discussed in chapter 5) oftentimes use the speech to introduce themselves to the nation while advocating on behalf of the candidate and trying to appeal to a specific cohort of voters. Most of the twelve modern spouses' speeches have contained background information about the speaker and the candidate, personal narratives designed to make the potential first couple relatable, and clear declarations about the nominee's fitness for office. Many others also address prominent political issues that are deemed feminine concerns (such as health care, education, child welfare, etc.). Alternatively, the speeches occasionally consider purportedly masculine topics from an ostensibly feminine point of view (e.g., discussing the economy by focusing on its impact on families). Some speakers have used the convention speech to outline the sorts of topics they intend to make part of their potential East Wing agenda.

Michelle Obama and Melania Trump each delivered a full, prepared speech at her husband's nominating convention. It was not surprising that Obama accepted the opportunity to address the nation. Her involvement throughout the primaries had made it clear that she did not shy away from the microphone and that she would welcome the chance to make her voice heard during a nationally televised event. In contrast, Trump's decision to participate was somewhat unexpected. Many politicos assumed Trump's alleged discomfort speaking to crowds would prevent her from taking the stage. Some speculated that she might do what Tipper Gore did in 2000 and prepare a prerecorded message in lieu of facing the large audience in real time.

In 2008, Michelle Obama was a noteworthy convention speaker. Even though she was not the first black woman to address a gathering of party delegates, she was the first to speak as a prospective first lady. Her speech largely fell in line with those of most contemporary candidates' spouses. Obama shared stories about her past, about life with her husband, and about the characteristics Barack possessed that would make him a good president. She presented a narrative that made her and

Barack seem like ordinary citizens who were placed in an extraordinary position. Obama used her speech to create bonds between herself, her husband, and American citizens by delineating shared values, telling tales of everyday life that many people would find familiar, and depicting herself as a competent and caring wife and mother.

Some online sources erroneously asserted that Melania Trump's 2016 RNC address was groundbreaking because she was the first naturalized citizen to deliver a spouse's speech at a convention, but that distinction actually belongs to Teresa Heinz Kerry due to her 2004 address. Trump's appearance was unique, though, because she was the first spouse of a major party nominee whose husband introduced her speech, and because she delivered the shortest prepared convention talk by a nominee's wife. Otherwise, Melania's address was fairly standard and contained many elements that have become expected parts of a mate's oration. She spoke about her past and the development of her values. She touted her husband's patriotism and his ability to lead the nation. She also vaguely outlined her interest in helping women and children. In most ways, the address was consistent with the orations delivered by the nominees' spouses who had addressed their respective conventions since 1992. Some critics argued that it was a little too much like one speech in particular.

Comparisons between Michelle Obama's 2008 DNC speech and Melania Trump's 2016 RNC address began with people across various media pointing out their similarities soon after Trump finished giving her speech. What started on social media with a few comments about the familiar content quickly led to charges of full-fledged plagiarism and side-by-side comparisons of the two speeches. Social and mainstream media sources maintained that Trump had lifted several passages from the Obama address and inserted them verbatim into hers. Because Trump had claimed to be the sole author of her speech prior to delivering the talk, questions about her morality, education, and values dominated coverage of the address. Scathing memes castigating Trump went viral. GOP operatives scrambled to explain away the passages, and eventually a purported ghostwriter was identified and scapegoated by Donald Trump's campaign staff. While the charge of plagiarism was quite serious, it failed to hold the mainstream media's attention for very long in a campaign filled with scandals and negative messaging. It did, however, become a significant part of social media discussions about Melania Trump, as several creative and biting GIFs and other posts cycled across various platforms for several weeks after the convention. This "borrowing" from Obama would continue to be problematic for Trump after she became first lady (see chapters 3 and 4).

Aside from the allegedly plagiarized content of Trump's 2016 oration, there were several other aspects of Michelle's and Melania's speeches that aligned closely with one another as well as with previous spouses' speeches. One comparable element was the way each woman defined herself. As is common in orations by nominees' wives, the women rely heavily on their connections to others to establish their identity. Michelle Obama begins her address by positioning herself "as a sister . . . as a wife . . . as a mother . . . and . . . as a daughter."[12] Melania Trump's self-depiction, while less succinctly stated, also depends heavily on her roles as a wife, daughter, sister, and mother. This portrayal is most evident in the sequential themes of her address; she starts by talking about her eighteen-year relationship with Donald, summarizes her parents' and sister's impact on her values, then explains how she tries to pass on these values to her son. Almost all spouses of nominees define themselves in this manner. Barbara Bush, Hillary Clinton, and Laura Bush all underscored their status as wives and mothers. Barbara Bush added her experiences as a grandmother, and Laura Bush also talked about being a daughter. Although defining themselves as wives makes sense (after all, they are speaking because they are married to the party's nominee), the additional relational links are simply a way for these speakers to reference customarily accepted roles for women in American society. This type of self-presentation is also a means for the women to create personas that many potential voters can relate to because most members of the audience are, have, or have had wives, mothers, sisters, daughters, etc.

Obama's depictions of her husband in her address stick more closely to the standard expectations of the spouse's convention speech than Trump's do. Obama very clearly tries to humanize Barack by sharing personal stories and providing intimate insights into his character. Trump, on the other hand, mostly praises her husband and bolsters his credentials in ways that offer no new revelations about Donald as a father or a husband. Obama tells listeners about her and her husband's early life. She also talks about their courtship and his response to the birth of their first child. Trump mostly speaks about her awareness of her husband's patriotism, his willingness to fight, and his leadership abilities. Obama conveys mildly deprecating but ultimately supportive anecdotes about Barack's idealism, determination, and motivation to help others. She also discusses his efforts to give his daughters "the affirming embrace of a father's love."[13] Trump mentions Donald's primary race victory on multiple occasions and makes general claims about his loyalty to others. Her only reference to him as a father is to say, "His children have been cared for and mentored to the extent that even his advisers admit they're an amazing testament to who he is as a man and a father."[14] It is notable that Trump never directly credits her husband for his skills as a dad—she never says who cared for or mentored his kids—and she relies on others' opinions to compliment him rather than sharing her own perspectives regarding his paternal contributions. All other past candidates' spouses who had children with their candidate-husband were almost boastful about how wonderful their mates were as fathers.

Melania Trump is, interestingly, more orthodox in her speech than Michelle Obama is when it comes to talking about patriotism and American ideals. The emphasis on patriotism is a common theme across all spouses' speeches at conventions, but Republican spouses tend to provide more overt demonstrations of how their love of country relates to the military and to notions of freedom and personal entrepreneurialism, whereas Democratic mates routinely focus on loyalty to fellow citizens and ideals associated with unity and fairness. In her speech, Trump talks a little bit about her personal history and highlights her patriotism in order to quell concerns about her as a foreign-born potential first lady. In the address, she briefly mentions her life in a communist country and outlines the various nations she visited as a model, but she expounds on her love for America and how she "cannot and will not take the freedoms this country offers for granted."[15] She also talks about the cost of liberty by highlighting the sacrifices veterans have made. Michelle Obama's 2008 address offers an unusual hybrid of ordinarily Republican and Democratic perspectives on patriotism by mixing gratitude for the military with appeals to unity and responsibility to others. Her speech blends the approaches by praising members of the armed services and acknowledging the sacrifices their families make; Obama frames supporting the military in a broadly inclusive manner. She also references a wide range of iconic moments in the history of the US to connect the past with the present and to underscore key values that undergird both the freedoms and responsibilities of American citizens. Obama's speech embraces the notion of love for and loyalty to the nation, but it is less partisan in its definition of patriotism than many past spouses' speeches.

In the end, the two speeches Michelle Obama and Melania Trump gave during the national conventions where their husbands first became their respective party's presidential nominee were attention-getting. Obama's speech earned mostly positive reviews. However, some conservative critics made generic complaints about her either overstepping the nebulous boundaries of propriety for a candidate's wife, a repeated refrain leveled against almost all politically active spouses from both parties, or they offered exaggerated readings of her liberalism that were not actually evident in the oration. Additionally, some liberal commentators argued that her address did not adequately reflect the groundbreaking nature of the position she was in and reprimanded her for embracing restrictive views of womanhood. Still, most remarks about Obama's 2008 DNC performance praised her poise, inclusivity, and ability to connect with diverse audiences.

Melania Trump's 2016 RNC speech will most likely be remembered not for her self-depictions and efforts to bolster her husband's credentials but for the accusations of plagiarism that dominated the coverage following its delivery. Conservative columnists downplayed the controversy and instead applauded Trump's demeanor and delivery. They commended her recognition of Bob Dole, an aging long-time party leader, and her emphasis on her and Donald's shared patriotism. Less generous reviews spotlighted the implications of her, a wealthy white woman, having appropriated several lines from Michelle Obama's address. Others complained that various aspects of her speech ran counter to the ideals and ideology her husband extolled. Online critics found fault with everything from her choice of dress to her accent and her seemingly exaggerated pauses. An objective assessment of Trump's address should acknowledge that while the plagiarism is inexcusable, the address itself did manage to meet several of the expectations for a campaign oration by a nominee's spouse. Though certainly not the best spouse's speech, Trump's address did, as future chapters demonstrate, effectively set the stage for her actions as first lady.

THE GENERAL ELECTION

Technically, the end of the nominating conventions signals the official start of the general election. However, the parties and candidates do not necessarily wait until that point to begin attacking one another directly, so an argument can be made that the functional start of the general election happens a month or two before the party gatherings. For the spouses, the turn toward the general election brings more sustained attention and higher expectations regarding their accessibility. The informal vetting process for potential first ladies becomes more intense when there are only two candidates remaining in the election, as it certainly did for Michelle Obama and Melania Trump.

Although they are routinely compared throughout presidential campaigns, the spouses of major party nominees are rarely placed in actual head-to-head competition. Unlike elected officials, the mates do not take part in debates or other confrontational engagements. However, since 1992, there has been one ritual encounter in which the two consorts are pitted against one another. This event is the quadrennial *Family Circle* magazine recipe contest originally dubbed the "First Lady Cookie Bake-off." When, during her husband's debut presidential campaign, Hillary Clinton made an offhand remark about not choosing to stay home and bake cookies, she sparked a controversy that spawned what was supposed to be a good-natured battle between the potential presidential helpmates. Clinton's oatmeal chocolate chip cookies unexpectedly beat out Barbara Bush's classic chocolate chip recipe. The contest ran again in 1996, and Clinton's same offering proved vastly more popular than Elizabeth Dole's pecan roll. Every spouse of a major party nominee has since provided an entry for the occasion.

In an odd historical twist, the *Family Circle* competition created a quirky point of similarity between Michelle Obama and Melania Trump. These two women were the only eventual first ladies to lose their initial recipe contest. In 2008, Michelle Obama offered a citrus shortbread cookie that lost to Cindy McCain's oatmeal-butterscotch treats. Controversy surrounded that match-up because McCain's entry was alleged to have originated from the back of a Hershey's box, but the result was still a loss for Obama. Eight years later, Melania Trump also lost her initial contest. She submitted what were called "Melania Trump's Star Cookies" to the newly renamed "Presidential Cookie Bake-off" and was beaten by Bill Clinton, who entered Hillary's previously successful cookie recipe. The 2016 battle also became tendentious when reporters questioned whether Trump had ever actually baked the cookies herself. No one asked the same of Bill Clinton, and no one seemed to care that his recipe was not original.

The cookie recipe contest is unique in that it is the only direct competition between mates of presidential nominees. However, it is not all that distinctive in that it, like most spousal activities, draws specific attention to talents and interests traditionally labeled feminine. The vast majority of general election events candidate spouses engage in are designed to highlight and evaluate attributes that fit orthodox female roles. In interviews, spouses are most often asked about their perspectives on motherhood and their relationships with their mates, and they are regularly critiqued for their fashion choices, hairstyles, and other ostensibly feminine traits. This certainly was the case with Michelle Obama in 2008 and Melania Trump in 2016. The routine nature of press coverage when it comes to candidates' spouses and the personas the women cultivated during their respective primary campaigns resulted in Obama and Trump being treated as caricatures of female stereotypes rather than complex and multifaceted women.

Throughout the 2008 general election, Michelle Obama enhanced the "everymom" image she developed during the primaries. Much like her predecessor Laura Bush did in 2000, Obama gave interviews that focused on her status as a mother, her concern for her daughters and for children generally, and her relationship with her husband. When Obama did talk about politics, she framed her opinions as those of a mother invested in making the future better for all children. She did not avoid criticism altogether, but she muted her discussions about race and focused on messages emphasizing hope, unity, and transcending difference. She told many stories intended to depict the Obamas as an average

American family dealing with the same struggles and experiencing the same joys as others. She contributed to the online family cookbook published by the campaign, talked about balancing the demands of life as a mother, wife, and campaign surrogate, and stressed the importance of being a good mother.

Obama frequently spoke about women's rights and touted women's skills and talents, grounding her arguments in her hopes for her (and everyone else's) daughters and their future. Because of her clever use of traditionally maternal frames and subtle but clear reasoning, Obama was rarely chastised for making what were assertive comments regarding women's empowerment. Unlike Hillary Clinton and Teresa Heinz Kerry, both of whom were reprimanded for promoting gender equality, Obama purportedly offered a more palatable point of view because she appeared to embrace traditional femininity herself while championing other women's ability to choose to be more heterodox. Overall, Michelle Obama remained quite vocal and active throughout the general election. She continued to build points of identification between herself and voters while she espoused her own perspectives and managed the stresses of public life.

During the 2016 general election, Melania Trump also largely stayed true to the persona she'd built throughout the primaries. She gave a few more interviews to members of the press, but she remained hushed at campaign rallies and continued to serve more as a background prop than an involved participant during events. She did take part in some of the more traditionally feminine activities expected of nominees' wives. In addition to sending a recipe to the *Family Circle* competition, she gave members of the press a tour of the Trump family's luxury apartment in New York City and talked about how she enjoyed motherhood and viewed it as her most important responsibility. When asked about her thoughts on potentially becoming the first lady, Trump's responses were usually positive but brief. Throughout most of the general election, Trump refrained from making many political remarks. However, in October 2016, she was forced into the limelight when a scandal that became known as "Pussygate" hit.

About a month before the 2016 election, Melania Trump confronted a situation oddly reminiscent of one Hillary Clinton faced in 1992 when Bill was accused of having had a long-term affair and Hillary chose to speak in his defense. A video was released that showed Donald Trump saying several offensive things and boasting about his derogatory view and treatment of women. In the clip, he brags that, because he is a star, he can just walk up to women and "grab them by the pussy."[16] In spite of the fact that she had been largely silent during the time between her RNC speech and the day the scandal broke, Melania Trump was relatively vocal in Donald's defense. She gave a series of interviews from her lavish apartment in which she repeated the explanation offered by her husband's campaign that the video contained so-called locker room talk that did not mean anything. Trump claimed that her husband was goaded into making such comments and argued that he actually had a great deal of respect for women. When pushed for examples of her husband's regard for females, Trump was not very forthcoming and instead repeated many of the seemingly stock phrases she'd used in her initial statements. Trump was widely criticized for her interviews, not because she was defending her husband (that would be expected of most political wives) but because the various exchanges with different journalists were so similar that it appeared she had simply memorized lines prepared for her by campaign staffers and had no original or authentic thoughts on the subject. Her sincerity was questioned, and her behavior reignited arguments about the mercenary nature of the Trump marriage.

Following her purportedly stilted defense of her husband's vulgar conversation about women, Trump received a flurry of mixed attention on mainstream and social media. Conservative outlets applauded the would-be first lady for her supportive actions and her understanding manner. A few right-wing reporters made direct comparisons between Hillary Clinton's defense of Bill and Melania's defense of Donald and were careful to point out that Hillary was excusing Bill's actual infidelity while Melania was merely explaining a misunderstood conversation. Liberal sources were much less positive, declaring Trump's defense hypocritical and damaging to women. Some commentators even argued that her acceptance of such an attitude by her husband disqualified her for the first ladyship because she could not condone such perspectives and still be an appropriate role model for American women herself. Across social media, Trump's response to her husband's remarks sparked discussions about whether the Republican candidate's wife was actually an abused and oppressed woman. Conspiracy theories spread about the degree of control Donald exerted over Melania, and some online observers began using the hashtag "#FreeMelania" to both reproach the GOP candidate and to urge Mrs. Trump to speak out on her own behalf. In an apparent rebuff of the criticism, shortly after the complaints emerged Melania Trump arrived at a presidential debate wearing a blouse adorned with what designers call a "pussy bow."

One big difference between the two situations Michelle Obama and Melania Trump faced in their respective general elections was that in 2008 Barack Obama enjoyed a fairly large lead over his opponent for the majority of the fall, but in 2016, Donald Trump's final victory was considered surprising by many. The differential in projected outcomes meant that as the apparent first lady-to-be Michelle Obama's general election performance was more heavily scrutinized than Melania Trump's was in spite of Trump's more scandal-filled campaign. Obama was queried more actively about her proposed agenda and was critiqued more fervently than many recent nominees' spouses. Questions about which issues she would champion were managed rather easily. She spoke about her interest in supporting military families and helping children live healthier lives, all the while cultivating a national mother persona. Obama also dealt with some extremely vicious and personal disparagements that came from opponents of her and her husband, many of which were based on her race and appearance (see chapter 4). GOP operatives, in an effort to erode support for the rather popular eventual first lady, charged Obama with being too black and acting too white. Social media trolls spread rumors that Michelle Obama had once been a man, pointing to her height to claim she was physically unladylike. Throughout the general election, Obama coped with these attacks primarily by ignoring them. Her decision not to respond to such derogatory denunciations became a strategy she used throughout her time as first lady.

Although Melania Trump was not perceived as an inevitable first lady near the end of the general election, some attention was still paid to her potential platform. In the waning days of the 2016 campaign, Trump gave only her second planned speech. The address, designed to help soften Donald's image and win support from undecided women, underscored Melania Trump's interest in helping children and vaguely outlined her intent to fight cyberbullying should she occupy the East Wing. While the speech itself was relatively well received, the fact that Trump's chosen topic of concern was directly at odds with her husband's behavior elicited a slew of new grievances. Mainstream and social media commentators almost immediately recommended that Trump's battle against bad online behavior should start at home. Memes and political cartoons highlighted the disconnect between Donald's aggressive Twitter attacks and Melania's stated disdain for such behaviors and implied that Melania had no influence over her husband. Coupled with additional remarks Melania Trump made in the final days of the election, in which she dismissed charges of actual sexual assault against her husband as lies intended to smear him, the speech produced a surge of laudatory responses from right-leaning news sources and disparaging assessments from left-wing pundits. The slight uptick in public activity by Trump near the end of the campaign did not seem to help her overall image in the minds of voters. Unlike most first-ladies-to-be, public opinion of Trump did not improve during the general election. Instead, more people held unfavorable views of her than favorable views from the delivery of her convention speech through Election Day and beyond.[17]

There were notable contextual similarities between the 2008 and 2016 presidential elections. Both contests witnessed more visible and vocal women than usual; the 2008 primary contenders included a competent and viable woman, the 2008 Republican vice presidential nominee was a female, the 2016 GOP primaries featured a female candidate, and the 2016 Democratic nominee was a woman. Conventional wisdom might suggest that with so many other women involved in the elections less attention would be paid to the spouses of the nominees. However, that was not the case either year.

Michelle Obama, by virtue of her active participation as a campaign surrogate, earned a great deal of coverage by mainstream and emerging media sources. She appeared on daytime and late-night talk shows and engaged with the public in more direct ways than many past presidents' spouses, particularly through mass messages sent by email and other online sources. Earning a mix of positive and negative responses, Obama cultivated a public image that gave citizens a clear sense of who she was politically and personally. Melania Trump was a more reluctant campaigner than her predecessor, giving only two public addresses and far fewer interviews than most modern candidates' spouses. Viewed mostly as a background prop during the primaries and a somewhat dubious defender of her husband during the general election, Trump did little throughout the 2016 campaign to endear herself to the American public and, instead, left the development of her public persona in the hands of a less-than-sympathetic press.

Although the two women were outwardly quite different in disposition and demeanor, they both experienced presidential campaigns in ways reminiscent of past would-be first ladies. Both women withstood the same types of scrutiny and borderline slander during the campaign that have been practiced since the early days of the republic. Obama was accused of being unladylike, just as Rachel Jackson had been, and Trump was charged with lacking the appropriate moral fiber to be first lady in much the same manner that Dolley Madison was. Like Laura Bush, both Obama and Trump gave convention addresses that advocated for their husbands, introduced themselves to the nation, and tried to demonstrate their connection to voters. Both women also managed controversies comparable to those Hillary Clinton endured. Obama's own words were used against her, just as Clinton's were in 1992; and Trump was placed in the awkward position of having to defend an indefensible spouse, just as Clinton was (again, in 1992). While participating in their husbands' campaigns, both women emphasized attributes tied to traditional femininity as major components of their public identities. The next chapter examines the challenges these women faced and the opportunities they embraced as each transitioned from being a candidate's spouse to first lady of the United States.

TWO

The Transition to the White House

Becoming First Lady

ONCE VOTE RESULTS ARE ANNOUNCED ON THE NIGHT OF MOST modern US presidential elections, speculation about the new administration begins. When a challenger wins the Oval Office, and shortly after victory and concession speeches are given, reporters and voters become eager for transition teams to begin their work. As the nation prepares for the peaceful exchange of power that is a hallmark of the American political system, adviser lists for the president-elect are developed, and people start thinking about potential appointments of cabinet members, ambassadors, and other consequential government posts. At the same time, members of the press and the public also start actively wondering about how the new White House matron will enact her position.

In 2008 and 2016, discussions about the potential approaches Michelle Obama and Melania Trump would take toward fulfilling their East Wing duties began in earnest as soon as their husbands were declared Electoral College winners. Obama and Trump each faced questions about what type of presidential consort she would be, how she would care for her school-aged offspring while in the media spotlight, and what roles extended families might play in the White House. The women's public personas were further shaped between election night and inauguration day as they prepared for life as first lady of the United States.

ELECTION NIGHT

The move from candidate's wife to presidential helpmate begins on the night of the election. In the modern era, winners and losers of presidential campaigns are announced by newscasters during what are usually hours-long media programs tracking the results of the national vote. Once an eventual winner is declared, pundits begin hypothesizing about various aspects of the upcoming administration on television, radio, and social media as audience members wait to hear from the contenders. Conversations about the wife of the president-elect frequently follow the candidate's victory speech; the spotlight is often literally and figuratively placed on the new first lady-to-be either during the address (if the winner thanks his wife) or as she stands dutifully by her husband when he takes or leaves the stage. For both Michelle Obama and Melania Trump, their election night participation and the attention it garnered was consistent with that of the general election; Obama was more active (although not vocal), Trump was more reserved, and both were critiqued for the clothing they wore.

November 4, 2008, was a historic night. Barack Obama became the first African American ever elected president of the United States. Polling had predicted the outcome well in advance of the vote count, so his triumph was not unexpected. Still, for many Americans it was an emotional night. When it came time for the new president-elect to address the nation, he and his family took the stage together and were introduced as "the next first family of the United States."[1] With Barack holding younger daughter Sasha's hand and Michelle holding Malia's, the Obama clan walked out toward the crowd, smiling and waving. Michelle was quite animated, laughing and chatting with her husband as they greeted the cheering crowd. After several minutes, Michelle Obama kissed her husband then took the girls backstage as the new president-elect began his speech. Obama returned at the end of the address and remained on stage with her husband for several minutes. Throughout the evening, the Obamas were in close physical proximity to one another and engaged in quite a bit of publicly appropriate affectionate contact—occasionally kissing, hugging, holding hands, and placing their arms around each other's waists. At the end of the evening, Barack and Michelle left the stage arm-in-arm. The family-oriented introduction and various interactions between Barack and Michelle on election night supported established narratives about the couple, depicting them as a somewhat conventional set of partners (where the wife cares for the kids and supports the husband) and a sincerely loving couple.

The 2016 presidential election occurred on November 8. Based on polling data released before ballots were cast, the final tally was a surprise to many. Although he lost the popular tally by almost three million votes, Donald Trump secured the Oval Office by winning 304 Electoral College votes. The close race led to a later-than-anticipated announcement of the projected outcome. Just before 3:00 a.m. Eastern time, Donald delivered his victory speech. After being introduced as "the President-Elect of the United States of America," Donald led a single-file line of family members and staffers onto the stage. Immediately behind him were Barron (his youngest son), Melania, his older children and their spouses, and a host of campaign staff and guests. As they entered and navigated the room, there was no direct communication between Donald and Melania Trump. As the entourage occasionally paused to wave at the cameras and crowd while walking toward the lectern, Melania turned to viewers and smiled momentarily as she waved, but her countenance dropped when she turned away from the camera. After his address, Donald gave his wife a brief kiss on the cheek as he passed along the line of people who'd joined him on stage. He dispensed hugs, handshakes, pats on the shoulder, and occasional kisses to others. Many such exchanges appeared more heartfelt and amiable than the one with his wife. The procession line then followed Trump off of the stage and into the crowd. As Donald talked with supporters, Melania spirited Barron away without a word to her husband. The fact that the speech occurred in the early hours of the morning could account for the lack of outward affection between the members of the eventual first family. Still, the event added to existing speculation regarding the business-like nature of the Trump marriage. When rumors later surfaced claiming that Melania was upset by her husband's win, pundits interpreted her lackluster performance and negligible contact with Donald as signs of marital trouble between the two.

In the days after their respective election night appearances, the press and the public commented quite a bit about each of the soon-to-be first ladies and the outfits they donned on their husbands' big night. In 2008,

Michelle Obama wore a red and black scoop-necked sleeveless sheath dress with a black cardigan sweater. While a few people applauded her decision to wear an outfit by an American designer, general reactions to the ensemble were not kind. Numerous news sources declared the dress "an eyesore,"[2] "less than flattering,"[3] and a "saturnine fashion misstep."[4] Michelle Obama's sartorial choice became such a widespread topic of conversation that public opinion pollsters even measured responses to the dress.[5] Additionally, some commentators berated Obama for her decisions regarding her daughters' clothing, assuming that she personally selected all of her family members' outfits. In many assessments, the attention Obama received regarding the dress overshadowed the fact of her historic standing as the first black woman slated to occupy the White House as first lady—though many such stories did follow in the months between election night and the inauguration.

Melania Trump wore a white silk, one-shoulder, half-sleeved, wide-legged jumpsuit to her husband's election night speech. Much like Obama's red and black dress, Trump's white jumper drew a great deal of media attention. However, the observations were dramatically different. Trump's sartorial choice was widely applauded as flattering and fashionable. Still, its color and cost led some analysts to critique the Ralph Lauren piece. Trump's decision to wear white, a color associated with women's suffrage (a fact much ballyhooed after Donald Trump's rival, Hillary Clinton, dressed in a white pantsuit for the final presidential debate), raised eyebrows among many writers, some of whom asked if Trump was trying to send a coded message with her attire. Pundits debated whether Trump was being clever in some way, or if perhaps people were reading too much into her clothing. What was less disputed was the $4,000 price tag for the jumpsuit. Several commentators pointed to its cost as an indicator of Trump's aloof nature and profligate ways and some claimed the outfit signaled that the first lady-to-be had no desire to connect with her husband's working-class base of supporters. Discussions about Trump's election night look were short-lived, and no opinion polls were conducted regarding it.

Michelle Obama and Melania Trump had both been compared to Jacqueline "Jackie" Kennedy for their usually on-point sartorial selections throughout their initial presidential campaigns. On election night, that connection was made once again. For Obama the link to the former first lady was disputed, while for Trump it was reinforced. In addition, less favorable parallels were made between Trump and Nancy Reagan, who had earned recrimination for her expensive tastes. Though Obama's clothing choice was heavily critiqued, some favorable associations were made between Obama and women like Pat Nixon and Rosalynn Carter because of their jovial election night appearances with their families and their affectionate interactions with their husbands. These various links to past first ladies were attempts to anticipate just what type of first lady Michelle Obama and Melania Trump would become.

INCOMING-OUTGOING FIRST LADY MEETINGS

One event that usually occurs during the early weeks of the presidential transition period is the initial visit the president-elect and his wife make to the White House. The gathering is designed to showcase the peaceful exchange of power between presidents and the enhanced status of their wives. Historically, the spousal visit has been instigated by an invitation from the sitting first lady to the incoming presidential mate. The purpose is to help the next occupant familiarize herself with the presidential residence and staff.

Although the private home tour is supposed to highlight the graciousness of the sitting first lady, not every helpmate has been eager to assist the person who superseded her. Perhaps one of the most notoriously strained spousal encounters occurred in late 1960. Mamie Eisenhower was said to have put off her meeting with Jacqueline Kennedy because she dreaded leaving the White House and lamented handing the residence over to a Democrat. She also allegedly disdained Kennedy, often referring to the young mother not by name but as "the college girl."[6] The two finally convened at the White House in early December, shortly after Kennedy had given birth to her son via a caesarean section. Eisenhower purportedly gave Kennedy a ninety-minute private tour of the residence (during which she never afforded the new mother an opportunity to sit) and failed to offer the use of a wheelchair requested by Kennedy's doctor.[7]

The 1960 get-together was not the only spousal visit to underscore the occasionally strained relationships between the women of the White House. After her husband lost his bid to remain in the Oval Office, Betty

Ford was said to have no interest in greeting Rosalynn Carter and can-celed two scheduled White House tours. The president-elect had to in-tervene on behalf of his wife to arrange a meeting. Ford later explained her hesitation by claiming, "No matter who follows you, you know they didn't deserve to be there."[8] Four years later, after struggling to accept the results of the 1980 election, Carter had a notably abbreviated walk through the residence with Nancy Reagan. Even though it makes sense that spouses of losing incumbents and members of the opposite party might hold grudges against their successors, not all stressful interactions are due to partisan-based hard feelings. When George H. W. Bush won the presidency as Ronald Reagan's incumbent vice president, Nancy Reagan did not extend an invitation to Barbara Bush until several days before the inauguration. Reagan and Bush had long been estranged, and many reports indicated that Bush barely set foot in the White House during the eight years her husband served as vice president, so it was no surprise that Reagan put off the tour.

Not all first lady meetings have been as vitriolic as those outlined above. In 1992, after the incumbent lost his reelection bid, Barbara Bush and Hillary Clinton had a reportedly pleasant conversation that was said to have spawned a deep mutual regard between the two. Clinton and Laura Bush were also rumored to be quite friendly with one another in 2000 in spite of the fact that their tour was significantly delayed. Unlike other postponements, the late Clinton-Bush scheduling was due to a heavily contested election and not personal ill will. The electoral winner was declared in mid-December, and one week later Clinton guided Bush through the White House in an amiable manner.

In November 2008, Laura Bush invited Michelle Obama to tour the White House. The exchange was described as very cordial, and Bush was deemed a gracious hostess. Although the event was private (Bush shooed away Obama's assistant who'd been brought along to take notes), the stories that emerged about the discussion asserted that the two were very chatty. According to some accounts, the women conversed at length about the challenges of motherhood and Bush offered Obama advice about raising daughters in the White House; she even recommended particular bedrooms for the Obama girls. The two also talked about carving out time for themselves and managing the very public life neither of them had sought. In addition, in a somewhat new tradition, Bush showed Obama the one window in the residence from which it was possible to view the Rose Garden and the Oval Office—a discovery Barbara Bush shared with Clinton who in turn pointed it out to Laura. By all accounts, Bush and Obama got on quite well for the duration of their visit.

After Donald Trump won the presidency in 2016, many people were curious what would happen during the face-to-face encounter between Michelle Obama and Melania Trump. While neither woman had established a reputation for aggressiveness or inhospitableness, behaviors by each during the 2016 campaign led to speculation that there would be tension between them. Throughout the election, Obama was a vocal proponent of Hillary Clinton and an open critic of Donald Trump. Obama never directly attacked Melania and did not engage in any inappropriate public personal haranguing of Donald, but she did make many assertions about the Republican candidate's lack of fitness for the presidency and about his questionable morals. Such protestations about a potential Trump presidency could not have gone unnoticed by Obama's invited guest.

One of the biggest reasons the press and the public showed particular interest in the conversation between Michelle Obama and Melania Trump was because of Trump's purported plagiarism of Obama's 2008 convention speech. When the similarities were discovered, Obama remained silent about the controversy even though other prominent Democrats scolded Trump for stealing the first lady's words and for denying having committed the offense after the fact. At no time did Trump acknowledge her error, nor did she publicly apologize to the first lady. Thus, many journalists wondered whether Obama might confront Trump about the speech during the tour. Because the media anticipated a somewhat frosty dialogue, the planned event received more attention than usual.

When the two did meet on November 10, 2016, there seemed to be some uneasiness between them but not the sort of animosity reporters expected. Obama and Trump had tea as they sat for photos together. Upholding traditions of the past, the tour occurred in private with no aides or reporters in tow. A statement released by the White House explained that the women talked about the challenges of raising children and about some practical aspects of negotiating life in the nation's capital. There was no word on any discussions regarding the campaign, nor was there any indication that either woman showed antipathy toward the other. The women completed their walk-through of the residence by joining their husbands in the Oval Office.

Because there were no outwardly contentious moments in the public time Obama and Trump spent together, the press had to find other things to write about regarding the meeting. Most journalists took the opportunity to remind readers about the misdeeds of the incoming first lady by focusing on her alleged plagiarism. Others turned to an age-old, go-to topic when it comes to presidential mates and wrote about the wardrobe choices each made. Of particular interest to some was Trump's decision to wear a sleeveless black dress after so much had previously been made about Obama occasionally baring her arms. Like the queries about Trump's white election night outfit, mainstream and social media sources asked whether Trump's choice of dress for her first White House visit was an attempt to make some sort of political or social statement. Others simply outlined the hypocrisy of criticizing Obama's exposed arms but ignoring Trump's.

Michelle Obama and Melania Trump met the expectations for a gracious exchange between first ladies set by Barbara Bush and maintained by Hillary Clinton and Laura Bush. Although there were plenty of personal and political grounds for at least some tension between the women, they transcended the nastiness that was a hallmark of the 2016 campaign and engaged one another in a manner befitting the position of first lady. Of course, initial reports about the interactions between Eisenhower and Kennedy made that visit seem more convivial than it was later revealed to have been, so there may yet be tales to tell about Obama and Trump's private conversation.

ANTICIPATING EVENTUAL FIRST LADYSHIPS

In November and December of 2008, Michelle Obama was a particularly popular subject among reporters and the public. Commentators across all forms of media spent a great deal of time speculating about America's first black national matriarch. Stories were published in various venues that reminded readers about Obama's past, including her upbringing, her academic achievements, and her professional success (the latter in vague terms). One recurring theme in the early days of the transition was Michelle Obama's impact on perceptions of modern American motherhood. Some stories credited her with redefining the concept of the working mother, while others argued that her new life as the first lady would alter what it meant to be a stay-at-home mom. Several articles also reinforced the idea of Obama as an ideal wife. The *New Yorker, Guardian,* and other outlets framed the new presidential couple as having a loving partnership in which Michelle provided much-needed and appreciated support for her ambitious but caring husband. A *Vanity Fair* feature on Obama framed her as a smart, talented woman and a deferential, loyal, and committed wife in an egalitarian marriage.[9] Although many articles acknowledged Obama's unique attributes, most accentuated the more traditional components of her life and style as they tried to determine what type of first lady she would be.

Media depictions of Obama during the transition were largely, but not entirely, positive. Some outlets praised her looks and applauded her healthy figure (particularly her arms), but others chided her purportedly imposing physique and lamented her tendency to occasionally go sleeveless. Similarly, just as some sources commended her for having established a career of her own, others condemned her for emasculating her husband by earning a higher salary than he had. When she formally resigned her position at the University of Chicago Hospitals just days before the inauguration, the news coverage was laudatory, praising her for putting her family and her duty to the nation ahead of her own career ambitions.

In addition to gender-based criticisms, opponents made racially charged critiques about Obama's potential influence as first lady. Some complained about her appearance, others about her background, and still others about her presumed attitude. Most were displays of ignorance and intolerance that served as reminders that electing a black man president of the United States did not mean racial equality had been achieved. However, a series of sympathetic articles were also published that highlighted Obama's unique experiences as a black woman in America. One piece explained how her self-reliance and individual successes were emblematic of expectations for many women of color who, for various reasons, are often the primary breadwinners in their families. Though it acknowledged the sacrifices Obama would have to make as first lady, including giving up certain freedoms and points of identity, the article painted her as an iconic representative of women of color and portrayed her relinquishment of certain aspects of herself as the price many women pay to gain power through assimilation and to open opportunities for others.[10] Despite the fact that there were several negative stories written about Obama, the press seemed inclined toward supporting the new feminine face of the White House.

Discussions about Melania Trump's potential role as first lady expanded following the election of her husband. Her speech about possibly championing a fight against cyberbullying received a bit of renewed attention in the days after the Electoral College projections were announced. However, because Trump had been clear during the campaign that she was not interested in impacting social or political policies, the majority of stories about her were less concerned with which issues she would address as the first lady than with introducing her to the nation and discussing her potential as a fashion influencer. Several articles written about Trump in early November recounted her life in Slovenia, her modeling career, and her courtship with Donald. A few talked about her as an accomplished businesswoman and a budding philanthropist. Even though some stories about Trump did underscore her standing as a mother and her desire to concentrate on raising Barron, there were no articles about how her enactment of motherhood while serving as first lady might influence perceptions of maternity.

One stark difference in the transition coverage of Trump and Obama was how the media used the women's marriages to understand the women and their eventual first ladyships. Unlike the idealized relationship between the Obamas, the Trumps' union was treated either as some type of business arrangement or as a throwback to the days when men acted as domineering providers and women as submissive nurturers. Tales about the Trumps' courtship routinely focused on how she benefited from her connection to the famous real estate developer and showman by gaining improved modeling opportunities and an upgrade in her lifestyle. Very few reports depicted their relationship as one of loving partners. The marriage was at best portrayed as mutually beneficial and at worst as an abusive situation. One online source deemed Trump the nation's "first victim," asserting that Melania was effectively trapped as the wife of the soon-to-be "bully-in-chief" Donald.[11] While the mainstream press did not initially repeat this particular characterization, many social media sites did make similar arguments, and memes with pictures of a seemingly oppressed Melania Trump circled the web.

During the transition, the public personas of both Michelle Obama and Melania Trump were mostly reinforced versions of those established during their presidential campaigns. There was, however, some broadening of the comparisons made between the future first ladies and their predecessors as each prepared to occupy the East Wing. The go-to link was always to Kennedy; Obama was frequently referred to as the black Jackie O (Kennedy's nickname after her marriage to Aristotle Onassis), and Trump was aligned with Kennedy because of her fashion savvy and aversion to campaigning. However, during the fall of 2008 and 2016, new connections to past presidential consorts emerged. As Obama toured schools for her daughters, reporters likened her to Rosalynn Carter and Hillary Clinton. When stories surfaced about Trump's hesitation to assume the first lady mantle, commentators quickly made references to other reluctant first ladies, as far back as Martha Washington.

In an effort to anticipate the type of first ladies Michelle Obama and Melania Trump might become, journalists asked Obama and Trump whom they viewed as role models. Because Obama did not readily provide a list of previous matriarchs as others had in the past (Clinton famously embraced Eleanor Roosevelt, Laura Bush praised her mother-in-law, etc.), reporters drew their own parallels between Obama and others based on particular characteristics. Many such efforts seemed a bit forced. They equated Obama with Clinton based on their educations and professions, but Obama's focus on motherhood rather than policy advocacy disrupted the parallel. The Kennedy association was also apt but limited since Obama had proven herself a much more enthusiastic political figure than the former first lady.

Melania Trump made it easier for pundits to associate her with past first ladies. Back in 1999, when her then-boyfriend Donald Trump first contemplated a presidential run, she listed Jackie Kennedy and Betty

Ford as potential role models.[12] Trump contended that the two women embodied an appealingly traditional perspective regarding the duties of a presidential helpmate. Once she was preparing to reside in the White House, political analysts revisited Trump's professed desire to emulate those women. Even though her admiration for the two was based on their supposed embrace of customary femininity, reporters used different attributes of the women to speculate about Trump's future. Because Kennedy traveled extensively during her short time in the White House, some writers assumed Trump would make goodwill trips abroad a large part of her agenda as well. Journalists also wondered whether Trump might remodel the White House as Kennedy had—this led to many comic representations of the president's residence wrapped in gold leaf much like Trump's New York City apartment. The assessments of Trump molding herself in the image of Betty Ford were more complex. These explications pointed out Ford's feminist perspectives, including her advocacy for equal pay and a woman's right to control her own body. Some politicos suggested that Trump might be secretly harboring more liberal perspectives than her husband, while others simply assumed Trump lacked a nuanced understanding of the women.

Critics of Trump's listed role models offered additional, and usually unflattering, alternatives. One of the more prominent suggestions was Nancy Reagan. Commentators likened the soon-to-be first lady to Reagan by depicting them both as manipulative women who altered their own perspectives to please their president-elect husbands. Journalists also drew parallels between Reagan's and Trump's extravagant spending and said both were out of touch with the American people. Reporters also linked Trump to Louisa Adams (because they were both born outside of the United States), Laura Bush (for her deference to her husband), and Michelle Obama (as a fashion icon).

SPECULATING ABOUT FAMILY INFLUENCES

During the transition period the press and the public also spend time considering the ways family members might engage in White House activities. While minor children such as Malia, Sasha, and Barron are certainly part of the story, adult children of the president as well as extended family members like grandparents, aunts, uncles, and others sometimes draw attention as potential players in the public or private dynamics of the new administration. Oftentimes, these discussions of family reflect back (positively and negatively) on the incoming first lady.

As the Obama family prepared to move to Washington, DC, much was made about the fact that there would be children in the White House once again. It had been almost a decade since Chelsea Clinton spent her tween and teenage years there and even longer since more than one minor resided in the East Wing. During the autumn of 2008, various newspapers and online sources published historical pieces about past presidential children and their influence. Old pictures of the Kennedy kids playing in the Oval Office circulated through mainstream and social media. Adult children of past presidents called for the news media to respect the Obama girls' privacy and implored the public to avoid critiquing the children. Those pleas did not prevent disparaging comments from people who opposed Barack Obama and from some mean-spirited individuals. Several attacks were based on practical complaints such as the taxpayer-supported funding of Secret Service details for the children. Others were implicitly race-based objections, calling the Obamas' life in the White House a form of subsidized housing and claiming that the Obama children were essentially on a high-priced form of welfare (a charge not leveled against white past presidents and their families). More personal attacks on the children tended to focus on their clothing, their hair, and their manners. However, the majority of the directly stated grievances were targeted toward Michelle Obama; she, as their mother, was held responsible for any perceived misstep on the part of her daughters in a way that their father was not.

During the fall of 2008, commentators began to anticipate how Michelle Obama would balance the responsibilities of motherhood while fulfilling her duties as the first lady. Reporters pointed to Obama's experience as a working mom to highlight her skill at multitasking. They also explained that a great deal of her success managing her professional and familial obligations in private life was possible because of her strong ties to her family members and their willingness to help out by occasionally watching the girls. Looking to the support network Obama utilized before and during the campaign, journalists began asking about her plans for developing a similar system in the White House. Shortly thereafter, the Obamas announced that Marian Robinson, Michelle's mother, would move to Washington, DC, and serve as a caretaker for her granddaughters.

Dubbing Robinson the "first granny,"[13] members of the press treated news about the addition to the first family in a mixed manner. Some observers commended the decision as a consequential recognition of the importance of family structures and as a nod to traditional multi-generational familial living styles once common in the United States. Others claimed the move was indicative of Barack Obama's efforts to put everyone on the government dole and that the grandmother's inclusion as part of the first family would come at a significant cost to taxpayers. Some politicos used the announcement to criticize Michelle Obama by arguing she was too enamored with her newfound fame to be bothered with raising her own children. Thus, before the Obamas even moved into the White House, they encountered a range of compliments and complaints about the various family members who would reside in the president's house.

Throughout the transition period following the 2016 election, the potential duties and impacts of the president-elect's family members were a much more prominent and complex topic than in 2008. One reason for the extensive discussions was the multifaceted nature of the Trump family. While Donald and Melania's young son, Barron, would certainly live with his parents, Donald also had adult offspring who had been intricately involved in his business dealings and his presidential campaign. Journalists asked about which children would maintain the business and which might take on duties in the White House.

As reporters squabbled about the various assignments Donald Trump Jr. and Eric Trump would be given relative to their father's business dealings and explained the legal necessity to build barriers between the Trump organization's corporate interests and the political influence of the Office of the President, other controversies were being manufactured regarding the more personal side of the Trump family's transition into the White House. In late November, followers of the first lady who expected a statement regarding her selection of a Washington-area school for Barron instead received notice that the wife and youngest son of the president would remain in New York City for five months following the inauguration. The official explanation proffered was that Melania Trump did not want to disrupt Barron's schooling, but the press and social media commentators attributed the decision to Trump's lack of enthusiasm for her new role. Three distinctly unflattering themes emerged in the reporting about her delayed move. Some stories framed the action as a convenient way for Trump to avoid her husband. Others stressed the cost of Secret Service details to fortify Trump Towers. There were also articles suggesting that Ivanka Trump would replace Melania as the White House matron. All three oft-repeated claims negatively impacted perceptions about Trump.

The idea of a first lady not joining her husband immediately following his inauguration seemed disconcerting to many pundits. Whereas a few predominantly conservative sources praised Mrs. Trump as a good mother and wife who chose to care for the family so her husband could focus on his job, most reports challenged the decision and portrayed it as an unprecedented move. History does not support such assertions. While most modern first ladies have joined their husbands immediately, many past presidents' spouses did not. Martha Washington waited four months before moving to be with George. Abigail Adams missed John Adams's inauguration ceremony and delayed her relocation because she was caring for her ailing mother-in-law. Anna Harrison, wife of William Henry Harrison, skipped her husband's swearing-in events, intending to move into the White House shortly thereafter. However, her husband died of pneumonia (contracted the day he became president) before she made it to Washington.

The twentieth-century norm was for wives to join their husbands, but not all remained in the White House full-time. Bess Truman spent more days in Missouri than in DC during Harry's presidency. Jackie Kennedy also passed much of her time as first lady outside of the White House. In two and a half years, she traveled—both as a goodwill ambassador and for pleasure—to multiple countries, including France, Switzerland, Italy, India, and Pakistan. There were also some stories that Michelle Obama had briefly considered remaining in Chicago so her daughters could finish their school year before establishing themselves in Washington. Clearly, Melania Trump's choice to remain in New York City for the first part of her husband's presidency did not follow the contemporary norm, but it was far from unprecedented.

Trump was clear that she would fly to DC to fulfill her obligations as the first lady whenever needed, yet the press continued to speculate that Ivanka Trump, Donald's eldest child, would act as the de facto first lady in the White House. As they rushed to judge Melania (for being unwilling to perform her duties) and Ivanka (for seeking power not rightfully belonging to her), many journalists overlooked the long history of women acting as surrogates for first ladies. Dolley Madison frequently stood alongside the widower Thomas Jefferson and served as his White House hostess for official social gatherings. Harriet Lane, niece of James Buchanan, fulfilled many of the responsibilities typically assigned to the first lady while Buchanan, a bachelor, was in the Oval Office. Many aged or infirm spouses of presidents also had daughters, nieces, and even granddaughters stand in their place at specific events. In the late 1960s, Julie Nixon became a very visible and vocal defender of her father, in many ways augmenting efforts by her mother and temporarily borrowing the rhetorical power of the first lady.

Although Donald and Melania each denied that Ivanka would replace Mrs. Trump, members of the press were loath to believe them and contemplated the many ways Donald's eldest daughter might usurp her stepmother. One *Washington Post* story argued that Ivanka's longtime position as a business adviser to her father increased the likelihood that she would significantly influence policy development and cited rumors about the new first daughter staking out an office in the West Wing as evidence of her taking over duties that would traditionally belong to Melania—an odd claim given that the first lady's offices are customarily located in the East Wing. The piece tried to compare Ivanka's advocacy for certain social issues to the agendas of Laura Bush and Michelle Obama and linked her advisory role to that of Hillary Clinton in the early part of Bill's first administration.[14] The article asserted that Ivanka Trump would be the most powerful first lady in the history of the United States. The contention, predicated upon the assumption that she would really be a first lady, failed to recognize the distinctions between a surrogate and an actual presidential spouse—specifically, that a proxy faces far less scrutiny, has fewer restrictions placed on her, and is not in fact the first lady of the United States. A more telling analysis would have explored Ivanka Trump's potential power outside of the confines of a first lady lens and assessed her as a female adviser with special access to the president. However, because many reporters still seek simplified explanations regarding female influence on the presidency, most tried to interpret Ivanka Trump using the frame of the first ladyship, a gendered filter they were familiar with.

Because Ivanka had worked with her father in the real estate business for years, she was viewed as having his trust and loyalty as well as being able to manage him in ways others could not. While it is possible to argue that these are spousal qualities, they are also those of a business partner, a family member, or a close friend. Donald Jr., who shared many of the same attributes as his sister, was listed as a possible political adviser but never as a potential White House matriarch. Jared Kushner, Ivanka's husband, likewise was considered a frontrunner for an executive branch position but was never regarded as threatening to assume the first ladyship. The fact that minds turned immediately to Ivanka taking over for the first lady was entirely gender-driven and reflects a tendency to perceive women in politics in a very limited manner.

In an effort to discount the rumors about being essentially overthrown by Ivanka, Melania Trump shared new insights with various reporters about her role as an adviser to her husband. She maintained that Donald referred to her as "my pollster" during the campaign and that he often asked her opinion on various political topics.[15] This revelation ran counter to the depictions of her during the election as uninvolved and uninterested in politics. The change was a minor attempt to reshape Trump's public image by stating she had a private but impactful role in her husband's campaign. It was also a way to reinforce her persona as a traditional wife by staving off rumors of trouble in her marriage and a means for making Trump seem more intent on and capable of fulfilling the obligations of the first lady. The private adviser role is one frequently claimed by presidential consorts, particularly those who avoid publicly expressing their own political perspectives but don't want to appear disempowered. Bess Truman, Mamie Eisenhower, and Jackie Kennedy were all said to be intimate advisers who rarely expressed their policy opinions in public.

The influence of family on the presidency and the first ladyship has been a significant topic of discussion during the past two transition periods. While neither Michelle Obama nor Melania Trump did anything particularly innovative or unprecedented relative to their families, the press tried to make it look as though they were taking unusual steps by preparing to care for their children. Obama's inclusion of the "first granny" became a point of both commendation and disapproval, and Trump was disparaged for trying not to disrupt her son's life. For Obama, the criticisms faded quickly, but Trump battled significant recrimination well into her first ladyship, and the concerns that Ivanka would effectively usurp her still remained a theme of various news stories into her second year in the White House (see chapter 4).

INAUGURATION DAY

The installation of a new American president draws worldwide attention. From the swearing-in ceremony and inaugural address to the formal evening celebrations, the day provides many opportunities for the nation to observe its new leader and his or her spouse. Inauguration day officially marks the end of the transition period and the beginning of the new governmental administration. It also signals a change in the nation's social leadership as a new pair becomes the figurehead couple of the United States. The incoming first lady is usually a quiet but extremely visible part of the events, and everything from her clothing to her facial expressions to her first dance with the new president offers material for mainstream and social media analysis.

There are three distinct components of inauguration day that are of particular interest to the press and the public. The first is the ceremonial welcome to the White House. Before the official swearing in, the president-elect and his wife meet the outgoing first couple at the president's residence for a brief photo opportunity. The occasion does not include any formal comments but serves as a kick-off to the transfer of power symbolized throughout the entire day. In what has become a relatively new tradition, the incumbent first couple meets their successors at the north portico of the White House with a few private words, handshakes, and hugs. They then enter the residence for a breakfast or tea, the final affair for which the sitting first lady acts as the national hostess.

In 2009, George and Laura Bush welcomed Barack and Michelle Obama in a brief but congenial meeting. The incumbent and his wife awaited the arrival of the Obamas on the top step of the portico entrance. The Obamas' limousine pulled to a stop, and the president-elect met his wife as she rounded the back of the car carrying a gift for her predecessor. After a flurry of greetings, Michelle Obama handed Laura Bush a white box with a red bow. The couples then stood on the steps to have a photo taken before entering the White House. The exchange was brief, and not much was made of it other than a few remarks about the women's attire. In the totality of the day, it was a moment easily overlooked because of the historic proceedings that followed.

The same occasion eight years later became an unusual focal point for the media. Seeming to search for any opportunity to criticize the incoming first couple, reporters seized on a few awkward exchanges between the Trumps and the Obamas and used them to rebuff Donald and Melania. The censure started when the Trumps disembarked their armored vehicle dubbed "the beast." Donald immediately ascended the steps of the portico and started shaking hands with Barack and kissing Michelle on the cheek while his wife was still getting out of the automobile. Political analysts berated the president-elect for appearing self-centered and showing no regard for his wife. When Melania joined the group a few seconds later, the Obamas welcomed her warmly, but there was some confusion as Melania handed Michelle a gift and Michelle looked for somewhere to put it so the couples could take a photo together. Politicos seized on Obama's response. Some erroneously claimed the gift was unusual and unexpected (clearly it was not, because Obama had given a present to Bush eight years earlier), and others mistook the effort to get rid of the box as a sign of Mrs. Obama's dislike for Mrs. Trump. In contrast to many of the media assertions, the video from the

White House shows Michelle Obama and Melania Trump smiling and chatting in a manner similar to the interaction between the Bush couple and the Obamas in 2009.

The portico welcoming on inauguration day 2017 also started the day-long assessment of the sartorial choices by both the incoming and outgoing first ladies. Pundits commented positively on Melania Trump's choice of a powder-blue dress suit and high-collared jacket paired with matching pumps and gloves. Journalists asserted that it was reminiscent of a frock donned by Jacqueline Kennedy in 1961. Some commentators complained that the incoming first lady was trying too hard to connect herself to a beloved figure from the past, but most complimented the president-elect's wife on her fashionable but reserved look and argued that the outfit signaled her intent to embrace a traditional approach to her new role. Reporters also provided laudatory assessments of the exiting first lady. They praised Obama's red and black tweed dress by calling it "subdued and relaxed"[16] and a "last grand gesture to her fashion-adoring fans."[17] The women were compared for their contrasting styles and their choice of colors; Michelle wore GOP red, while Melania was clad in Democratic blue. (Later, at the swearing in, Trump, Obama, and Hillary Clinton—who wore white—stood together in what some writers called a "first lady American flag."[18])

The second component of the inaugural festivities heavily covered by various media is the ceremony during which the president-elect becomes the new commander in chief. This part of the day includes the swearing in of the president, the delivery of the new leader's inaugural address, and a parade from the Capitol building to the White House. Each step of the way, the spouse of the new president plays a prominent role. Since Lyndon B. Johnson's second inauguration in 1965, every wife of the about-to-be president has held the Bible on which the new leader placed his hand as he took the official oath of office. The inclusion of the spouse is noteworthy because it symbolically underscores the person's helpmate role in the administration. The historic nature of Michelle Obama and Melania Trump each being a "first" to hold the Bible— Obama as the first African American wife of a new president and Trump as the first immigrant spouse to assist in the application of the oath—was acknowledged by a few news sources, but neither woman's actions dominated press coverage.

Following the ritual affirmation of the new president, the commander in chief customarily addresses the nation. The spouse generally stands or sits stoically in the background looking as though she is listening intently while her husband delivers his oration. Much like holding the Bible, the behaviors of a first lady during the speech are seldom commented upon. This was the case in 2009. Michelle Obama rarely appeared on camera, but when she did, she was usually looking toward her husband. In one or two frames she was checking on her young daughters, who were seated next to her, but those moments were not deemed troublesome or newsworthy.

In 2017, as Donald Trump delivered his inaugural address, Melania Trump sat with her son a few rows behind the lectern. Observers noted that she was not seated in the front row, and they commented on her son's fidgeting throughout the speech. After the ceremony was over, video clips from various parts of the event that showed Melania Trump scowling or shifting from smiling to frowning behind her husband's back circulated throughout several social and mainstream media sites. Journalists speculated about her change in demeanor and used the clips to claim that Donald had been brusque either with his son or wife during a national prayer. Rumors about the encounter were so widespread that fact-checking websites put out reports verifying the veracity of the video snippets but cautioning against accepting the proffered explanations for the change in her countenance. The video was later combined with other pictures and recordings of the new first couple to promulgate the idea that the Trumps' marriage was not a happy one.

Following the verbal rituals associated with taking the oath of office, there is customarily a recessional parade that runs from the US Capitol to the White House. Usually, there is not much to report from the spectacle unless something historic or uncommon occurs. On March 4, 1841, William Harrison contracted pneumonia when he refused to wear a coat during his inaugural address and afterward, while trotting his horse down the parade route; he died less than a month later, triggering the presidential succession clause of the US Constitution for the first time. In 1909, Helen Taft became the first presidential spouse to accompany her husband on the parade route when she rode with William in an open carriage. The 1977 procession was the first in which the new president walked the entire route. Jimmy and Rosalynn Carter skipped the motorcade and strolled along Pennsylvania Avenue smiling, waving, and shaking hands with folks. Since then, every new presidential couple has walked at least some part of the mile-long route.

The 2009 inaugural parade was well attended, and crowds cheered when Barack and Michelle Obama stepped out of their limousine and walked together for several blocks. Some reporters likened attendees' reactions to those of fans applauding a favorite rock star or movie icon and pointed out that the enthusiasm of those assembled seemed equally high for the first lady as for the president. Although a minor part of the day's reporting, the coverage reinforced the idea that the new president and his wife were both quite popular. Stories about the procession also spotlighted numerous displays of affection between Barack and Michelle—describing their close physical proximity throughout the walk as well as their tendency to hold hands, talk with one another, and laugh together—in a manner that underscored their image as a loving couple. The only reminder that admiration for the new first couple was not universal was a discussion about security concerns surrounding their walk.

In January 2017, coverage of the parade and the first couple's stroll was considerably less positive. Stories focused on the low turnout for the parade and the new president's decision to walk the section that included his namesake hotel. Reporters pointed out the jeering and heckling mixed in with cheers from the crowd. A few commentators maintained that Melania Trump looked uncomfortable and unnatural walking down the street in her pencil-cut skirt and high-heeled shoes, but most mentions of the new first lady were either neutral or complimentary. Some journalists did remark on the handful of affectionate moments between Donald and Melania as they walked together, highlighting the times they held hands and noting the infrequency of such public displays during the campaign. However, the positive reflections on their relationship that the handholding and occasional kiss on the cheek inspired were short-lived because the press contrasted these gestures against other, less gracious moments between the two.

The third element of inauguration day that receives a large amount of media attention is the series of celebratory evening events. This part of the day routinely focuses more on the new first lady than her husband. Although the women who have assumed this role are critiqued regarding their sense of style well before moving into the White House, their choice of attire for the evening's receptions is always of major interest. The day after the inauguration, alongside stories about the new leader's speech, there are invariably several articles about the first lady's ball gown that provide details about its cost and designer or that critique various aspects of the sartorial selection by the new White House matriarch. The amount of consideration given to her dress reflects the long tradition of viewing the first lady of the United States as a figurehead who represents the ideals of American womanhood by entwining conventional femininity and fashion savvy.

Past presidents' mates have been praised and rebuffed for almost every aspect of their inaugural ball attire. Mamie Eisenhower wore a pink dress because that hue was her favorite color. Reporters both applauded the first lady for her overtly feminine choice and faulted her for appearing too much like a little girl. Lady Bird Johnson chose yellow, a color said to represent hopeful optimism, for her outfit in 1965 and was likened to a nestling by critics alluding to her nickname. In 1992, Hillary Clinton wore a purple gown, reportedly to infuse her husband's presidency with a regal flair, but observers complained the color simply washed out her complexion. Many first ladies have opted for white or ivory, including Eleanor Roosevelt (in 1941), Jacqueline Kennedy, Nancy Reagan, Michelle Obama, and Melania Trump. The white, hand-beaded, one-shoulder sheath gown that layered lace over silk that Nancy Reagan wore for Ronald's initial inauguration was rumored to have cost over $22,000. It was a stark contrast to her predecessor Rosalynn Carter's off-the-rack dress (which she'd worn at least twice before) and netted Reagan a great deal of criticism. Ignoring the clamor about her first dress, Reagan chose as her second inaugural gown another white outfit from the same designer, with an estimated price of $46,000.

The first ladies' inaugural dresses are considered to be of such social and historical value that many of them are displayed in the Smithsonian's National Museum of American History. Curators began asking first ladies to donate garments the women felt best represented their style in 1912. Nellie Taft donated the gown she wore to the inaugural ball. All subsequent first ladies who attended an inaugural ball also gifted their dresses to the collection. Even though the initial practice was to display a donor's gown only after her time in the White House came to a close, when Mamie Eisenhower attended the opening of the First Lady's Hall of the museum, the administrators reconsidered their position and displayed her pink dress as part of the initial exhibition. In 1964, Lady Bird Johnson became the first to present her frock in a public ceremony, initiating a public relations opportunity that has since become something of a tradition that both Michelle Obama and Melania Trump followed.

In 2009, Michelle Obama selected a white dress made of silk chiffon to wear to the ten celebratory functions she attended on the night of her husband's inauguration. It was a one-shouldered ball gown accented with organza and Swarovski crystals. Obama was applauded both for the style of the dress and for promoting up-and-coming American designer Jason Wu by wearing his creation when she had many other couturiers' offerings to choose from. A few critics complained that the outfit looked unkempt because of its accent pieces, but Obama generally earned a great deal of acclaim and was, once again, heralded as fashion-forward and trendsetting. In addition to the compliments Obama received for her dress, she was also commended for her endurance and her displays of personality throughout the long night of celebrations. With ten dances and lots of mingling on the schedule, reporters averred that Obama remained cheerful, upbeat, and affectionate with her husband at each public appearance. From their first dance to their last, the Obamas were described as chatting, smiling, laughing, kissing, and holding hands all evening long. This positive attention reinforced the image of the Obamas as a devoted couple and of Michelle as a supportive wife.

The Trumps attended three inaugural balls on the night of January 20, 2017. To each, Melania wore an off-the-shoulder, white-silk-crepe column gown. The dress had a slit partway up her right thigh, an accent ruffle across the body, and a thin red belt around the waist. Journalists alleged that Trump had difficulty finding a designer, and some writers speculated that her husband's divisive campaign rhetoric and controversial win led several prominent couturiers to avoid having their names associated with the new administration. This was an unusual situation for Mrs. Trump who, as a former model and well-known woman, was a sought-after client for many designers. It was also odd because dressmakers routinely clamor to outfit the first lady in order to boost their own reputations and sales. Just over two weeks before the inauguration, the French-American designer Hervè Pierre agreed to create the gown and worked with the fashion-savvy Trump, who requested a unique and modern-looking garment. Reviews of the dress were extremely complimentary. A few articles contrasted Trump's white look against Obama's, and a few others compared it with Reagan's two ivory garments. Described as youthful, crisp, and elegant, the gown was viewed as a positive choice and a stylish reflection of the new first lady's tastes.

The favorable coverage of Trump's dress was almost overshadowed by media efforts to once again call the nature of her relationship with Donald into question based on their interactions throughout the night. Although most first couples are not particularly acclaimed for their dancing skills, Donald and Melania were derogatorily likened to a "middle-school couple who tries to dance but just moves their feet in a circle and doesn't even look at the person they're dancing with."[19] Picking up on the recurring critiques of the stability of the Trump marriage, some critics asserted that Donald and Melania's stiff movements indicated a lack of regard between the two. The tenacity of the media's attempts to discredit the Trump union also led to stories that described their behaviors during particular songs in ways that implied a lack of intimacy between them. For example, several stories mentioned the fact that Donald and Melania began dancing with different partners midway through the song "I Will Always Love You" and that Donald conversed more with his vice president while dancing with Melania than he did with the first lady.

The day the spouse of a president-elect becomes the first lady is filled with events that focus particularly on the new president but also include opportunities for the new White House matron to earn either laudatory or disparaging public attention. Because it is the culmination of the transition period between election night and the start of the new administration, many of the established themes about a president's spouse affect interpretations of that consequential day. In the case of Michelle Obama, the press's tendency to treat her favorably led to an amplification of her positive qualities during the inaugural ceremonies and evening celebrations. For Melania Trump, the divisive nature of her husband's campaign, his contentiousness even in the face of victory, and her own minimal public engagement led to less flattering coverage of the couple and of Melania.

The transition period between election day and the presidential inauguration is obviously a pretty busy time for presidents-elect, but it is also an important time for their spouses. As wives of winning candidates, the women preparing to occupy the White House receive a great deal of concentrated attention during the months after the contest ends because they no longer share the spotlight with the mate of another nominee. During November, December, and January, the press and the public look for cues to help determine just what type of first lady the new national matriarch will be and often try to associate incoming presidential helpmates with those of the past in order to anticipate the pending first ladyship. Unfortunately, such attempts to predict future behaviors are problematic because they rely on partial information and make restrictive assumptions about the homogeneity of women.

Michelle Obama and Melania Trump endured heavy scrutiny during their respective transition periods as people tried to figure out how they would enact the role of first lady. Obama had to make many of the same efforts to reduce uncertainty surrounding her that previous incoming first ladies did, but because she was the first African American woman in this position, she also had to manage race-based anxieties others never dealt with. Fortunately for her, she had some clear advantages as her family prepared to move to Washington, DC, including her popularity, Barack's relatively dominant electoral victory, and the relatable "everymom" persona she had cultivated. Even though criticisms about her abounded between the day votes were cast and the swearing-in ceremony, Obama's well-established image as the consummate working mom quelled many (but not all) concerns about her probable impact as first lady.

Melania Trump faced a host of difficulties heading into the transition period. She was a former immigrant with a thick accent who rarely spoke on her own behalf and who was married to a tendentious president-elect who had lost the popular vote by almost three million ballots. Her lack of participation in the primaries and general election led to a problematic outward identity that did not create perceived bonds of consubstantiality with the public. Thus, when criticisms emerged during the transition period, attempts to curb concerns about the atypical first lady-to-be were not particularly successful. The aloof persona Melania had developed during the campaign led to questions about her willingness to be the first lady, and her actions during the fall of 2016 did little to quiet rumors that she intended to surrender the position to her stepdaughter. These problems plagued her throughout her time as the president's wife.

Although Michelle Obama's and Melania Trump's public personas were pretty deeply entrenched before their first full day in the White House, as the sitting first lady, each gained new opportunities to confirm and to contest those images. Throughout her years as the presidential consort, each took very different approaches to managing her role. The next chapter examines how these women solidified and challenged public perceptions about themselves after becoming the first lady.

First Lady Rosalynn Carter. *Courtesy of Library of Congress*

First Lady Barbara Bush reading to children in the Library of Congress Thomas Jefferson Building, Washington, DC. *Courtesy of Library of Congress*

Presidential nominee George H. W. Bush and wife Barbara Bush wave to the crowd at the 1992 Republican National Convention in Houston, Texas. *Courtesy of Library of Congress*

Librarian of Congress James H. Billington with First Lady Laura Bush and others at the opening of the first National Book Festival held on the East Lawn of the US Capitol.
Courtesy of Library of Congress

Laura Bush. *Courtesy of Library of Congress*

First Lady Hillary Clinton and President Bill Clinton at the 1997 dedication of the Franklin Delano Roosevelt Memorial in Washington, DC. *Courtesy of Library of Congress*

Above, Nancy Reagan at the White House. *Courtesy of Library of Congress*

Left, Nancy Reagan. *Courtesy of Library of Congress*

Above, Pat Nixon. *Courtesy of Library of Congress*

Left, Betty Ford. *Courtesy of Library of Congress*

Right, Lady Bird Johnson. *Courtesy of Library of Congress*

Below, First Lady Betty Ford shakes hands at a campaign stop in the South. *Courtesy of Library of Congress*

Jacqueline Kennedy, wife of President Kennedy, at opening of Philharmonic Hall, Lincoln Center, New York City on September 23, 1962. *ID 60352808 © Picturemakersllc | Dreamstime.com*

Facing, Jacqueline Bouvier Kennedy and John F. Kennedy cutting the cake at their wedding, September 12, 1953, Newport, Rhode Island. *Courtesy of Library of Congress*

Left, Martha Washington stamp. *Courtesy of iStock*

Below, Martha Washington. *Courtesy of iStock*

Above, Wedding of George Washington. *Courtesy of iStock*

Right, Dolley Madison. *Courtesy of iStock*

Martha Jefferson, wife of Thomas Jefferson, died nineteen years before he took office, leaving the widower with no first lady in residence. *Courtesy of iStock*

Frances Folsom Cleveland, wife of President Grover Cleveland, married the president one year into his first term in office. *Courtesy of iStock*

Rose Elizabeth Cleveland, sister of President Grover Cleveland, served as acting first lady until the president married Frances Folsom. *Courtesy of iStock*

Canceled stamp from India commemorating Eleanor Roosevelt and the Universal
Declaration of Human Rights. *Courtesy of iStock*

Canceled stamp featuring Eleanor
Roosevelt. *Courtesy of iStock*

A 1998 USA postage stamp with an
illustration of Eleanor Roosevelt (1884–
1962) meeting a young girl with flowers.
Roosevelt was the longest serving US First
Lady, from 1933–1945, and championed
many human rights and social issues before,
during, and after her role as first lady.
Stamp design by Paul Calle.
Courtesy of iStock

Above, A sidewalk vendor sells a variety of political and patriotic souvenirs in Washington, DC. *Courtesy of iStock*

Facing top, Democratic presidential candidate Hillary Clinton at a rally in Philadelphia, Pennsylvania. *Courtesy of iStock*

Facing bottom, Democratic presidential candidate and former Secretary of State Hillary Clinton campaigns at Nelson-Mulligan Carpenters' Training Center in St. Louis, Missouri. *Courtesy of iStock*

Gallery

First Lady Michelle Obama's official portrait.
Courtesy of Library of Congress

Melania Trump.
Courtesy of Library of Congress

Michelle Obama waves at the crowd from the viewing stand in front of the White House, Washington, DC, at the 2009 Inaugural Parade.

Courtesy of Library of Congress

Facing, Melania Trump attends *The Celebrity Apprentice* finale at Trump Tower on February 16, 2015 in New York, NY.

Courtesy of Alamy

Barack and Michelle Obama as confetti falls.
Courtesy of Alamy

Below, President Barack Obama, First Lady Michelle Obama, and their
daughters, Malia (*left*) and Sasha (*right*) sit for a family portrait.
Courtesy of Alamy

Donald Trump and Melania Trump at the 'Superheroes: Fashion and Fantasy' Costume Institute Gala held at the Metropolitan Museum of Art on May 5, 2008.

© Nancy Kaszerman/ZUMA Press. Courtesy of Alamy

Below, Melania Trump and Barron Trump on the Hollywood Walk of Fame, in Los Angeles, California, on January 16, 2007.

Courtesy of Alamy

Above, Michelle Obama runs at an activity station during a "Let's Move! London" event at Winfield House in London, England.

Courtesy of Alamy

Left, Melania Trump public appearance at QVC's Fashion's Night Out event, Suspenders Building in SoHo New York, NY on September 8, 2011.

ID 67680712
© *Dwong19 |*
Dreamstime.com

Melania Trump during visit in Poland with Donald Trump.
ID 99205326 © Maciej Gillert | Dreamstime.com

Below, First Lady Michelle Obama joins students for a Bollywood Dance
Clinic in the State Dining Room of the White House, Nov. 5, 2013.
Courtesy of Alamy

First Lady Michelle Obama participates in filming for the Animal Planet Puppy Bowl on the South Lawn of the White House on October 28, 2013 in Washington, DC.

Courtesy of Alamy

Facing top, Melania Trump on Day 1 of the Republican National Convention held at the Quicken Arena in Cleveland, Ohio, on July 18, 2016.

Credit: Bruce Cotler/Globe Photos/ZUMA Wire/Alamy Live News.
Courtesy of Alamy

Facing bottom, First Lady Michelle Obama greets crowd at President Obama campaign rally at Orr Middle School in Las Vegas, Nevada, on October 26, 2012.

Courtesy of Alamy

Above, First Lady Melania Trump (*right*) walks along the Colonnade
with Argentine First Lady Juliana Awada at the White House
April 27, 2017 in Washington, DC. *Courtesy of Alamy*

Facing top, First Lady Michelle Obama participates in her last White House
vegetable garden harvest on October 6, 2016 in Washington, DC.
Credit: Patsy Lynch/Alamy Live News. Courtesy of Alamy

Facing bottom, First Lady Melania Trump interacts with Ilana Jordan, a student at the Imagine
Andrews school at the youth center on Joint Base Andrews, Maryland, on Sept. 15, 2017.
The facility offers various programs such as before and after school care, social recreation,
sports and fitness, and instructional programs for more than 800 children.
(US Air Force photo by Senior Airman Jordyn Fetter). Courtesy of Alamy

Democratic presidential candidate Hillary Clinton and
First Lady Michelle Obama.

ID 85020855 © Joe Sohm | Dreamstime.com

President Barack Obama and Michelle Obama pose with President-
elect Donald Trump and wife Melania at the White House before
the inauguration on January 20, 2017 in Washington, DC, when
Trump became the 45th President of the United States.

Photo by Kevin Dietsch/UPI. Courtesy of Alamy

President Donald J. Trump, Melania Trump, former President Barack Obama, Michelle Obama, former President Bill Clinton, Hillary Clinton, and former President Jimmy Carter attend the state funeral service of former President George H. W. Bush at the National Cathedral on December 5, 2018 in Washington, DC.

Credit: Chris Kleponis / Pool via CNP. Courtesy of Alamy

THREE

Forging Their Own Paths

Michelle and Melania as First Ladies

ONCE THE POMP AND CIRCUMSTANCE OF INAUGURATION DAY ends, the press and public turn from speculating about the new occupants of the White House to evaluating them. On an almost daily basis, assessments are offered regarding the first lady and what kind of public figure she is. Even though the first lady of the United States does not hold an elected office, she—by virtue of being married to the president—is expected to serve the nation in ways that are not specifically delineated and that vary based on the social and political climate of the time. The job of presidential helpmate is unpaid (though it comes with several material benefits) and does not have a codified set of requirements or range of authority. The flexibility of the post suggests that each woman who assumes it has the opportunity to shape it and make it her own. However, in practice all first ladies face the challenge of operating within an undefined set of ever-changing constraints that restrict their behaviors and impact how their actions are perceived. Moreover, because each presidential consort acts (whether intentionally or not) as a role model for girls and women and is a purported exemplar of American femininity, all presidents' mates must manage intense scrutiny while building a life in an unusually public space.

The wife of a presidential nominee or even a president-elect has ample opportunities to cultivate a public image for herself, but the White House matron's ability to attract attention is substantially greater. There are always reporters and pundits ready to propagate the messages, dissect the behaviors, and evaluate the effectiveness of the president's spouse. The initial months of her first ladyship are often trying as the president's mate establishes how she will manage the position she has been thrust into by virtue of her husband's political success. The first year is particularly consequential because it sets the stage for her time in the public eye.

When Michelle Obama and Melania Trump each became the first lady, they confronted similar kinds of problems and opportunities. Both were relative newcomers to the national political stage, had personal histories that distinguished them from other presidential spouses, were well known for their fashion savvy, and had lower favorability ratings than the woman each replaced. Many of these attributes made both Obama and Trump particularly interesting to members of mainstream and social media, and the women had several chances to shape perceptions about themselves. The manner in which Obama and Trump managed their first ladyships reveals a great deal about their distinct public images.

THE OFFICE OF THE FIRST LADY

New first ladies (as opposed to those starting a second term) must learn to navigate the political and social expectations that are part of life as the nation's matriarch while also managing a new household, caring for their families, and figuring out how to maintain an individual sense of identity. In order to balance their responsibilities as a public figure and a private person, most modern presidential consorts work with both the semipermanent residential staff of the White House and a team of employees specifically selected to aid the president's mate. Domestic personnel who work in the residence generally remain in place as presidents and first ladies change; these staff members keep the national landmark that is the presidential home functioning. They are responsible for maintaining the household, and they ensure that the first lady does not need to spend too much time negotiating the day-to-day management of such a large and historic building. The matriarch of the White House once expended a great deal of energy directly overseeing the residential staff, but more contemporary first ladies face different demands that require multiple types of assistance.

Edith Roosevelt was the first president's wife to have a federally funded employee who was not part of the residential staff working specifically on her behalf. She hired Isabella Hagner as her social secretary in 1902. Hagner's job description soon expanded as she became a press manager for the first lady by controlling media access to the first family, distributing preapproved pictures of the first lady, and discouraging the publication of photos of the Roosevelt children. Subsequent first ladies continued the tradition of using governmental aides and, as the demands of the position grew, so did their staffs. In the 1970s, Rosalynn Carter's assistants were dubbed the "Office of the First Lady," a title that remains in effect today.

For many decades, every presidential consort has confronted a growing set of responsibilities, and presidential mates have a particularly onerous task as the highest profile unsalaried public servants in America. Still, the personnel paid to aid the first lady have routinely become a point of political contention. Michelle Obama and Melania Trump both raised eyebrows with their respective staffing decisions early in their tenure as first lady. Obama's staff came under scrutiny when critics argued that it was unjustifiably large and costly. News stories stated she had two dozen government employees working for her. Conservative outlets often inflated the number by including interns and private employees to assert that Obama's was the biggest and most expensive Office of the First Lady in history. Fact-checking organizations disproved these claims and explained that her group was average-sized for the era. Articles critical of Obama referred to her assistants as "servants" to pejoratively equate the first lady with royalty or to allude to Southern slaveholders. Right-wing commentators tied her need for help to alleged laziness and a desire to be pampered. Combined with rumors that Obama had racked up large room-service bills during the election and transition, opponents used the size of the Office of the First Lady to frame Obama as self-indulgent in an attempt to drive a wedge between the new White House matriarch and average Americans struggling through the Great Recession.

Melania Trump's decisions regarding her assistants were decidedly different from those of her predecessor. Shortly after the 2016 inauguration, the White House announced that Trump would decrease the number of employees dedicated to the Office of the First Lady. Touted as an effort to reduce the bloated staff built by Obama and to save the taxpayers money, the move was intended to demonstrate Melania's thriftiness and her willingness to be in more direct control of her own activities. However, the public and the press generally did not interpret the move as the Trump Administration had planned. Instead, critics pointed to the fact that Melania Trump was still residing in New York City as the reason she did not need a large Washington-based staff and asserted that the additional cost for Secret Service personnel to secure Trump's apartment building exceeded the purported savings from fewer East Wing office workers. In addition, journalists used the lack of a sizeable support system as evidence of Trump shunning her new role. Even though the small staff was supposed to create a positive perception of Trump, it only did so among audiences already sympathetic to the first lady. One year later, as she prepared to launch her social agenda, Trump quietly increased the number of people working for her.

The need for a supporting cast of workers to manage the personal and public needs of any president's mate is understandable based on the expectations the person must meet. As first ladies have been pressured to maintain an increasingly public profile, they have needed more and more assistance from residential and office personnel. Regardless of the increasing workload, the Office of the First Lady still incites scrutiny. The hypocrisy of the public's desire for an active first lady but reluctance to give her the resources to be one causes problems for all women who oversee the East Wing—and this was certainly the case for Michelle Obama and Melania Trump.

THE DUTIES OF THE FIRST LADY

It is clear that a modern White House matron needs assistance negotiating the assorted responsibilities thrust upon her. Less obvious is what exactly the nation expects the president's mate to do. In spite of the lack of a serviceable job description, all first ladies are pressured to undertake actions that, while distinct in their specific details, are categorically consistent across time. In addition to their personal duties as wives and mothers, first ladies are responsible for acting as the nation's hostess, engaging as a social advocate, and being the compassionate face of the administration in times of crisis. The ways Michelle Obama and Melania Trump negotiated these commitments during their early years in the White House impacted how the public and press interpreted the women.

NATIONAL HOSTESS

The country's most visible political spouses are regularly tasked with fulfilling ceremonial obligations, serving as event planners, and being gracious entertainers. As the nation's hostess, the president's wife is called upon to be a welcoming figure who embodies warmth and elegance. She is asked to be an amiable and relatable person who maintains a sense of propriety and a hint of nobility. As a behavioral model for other women, the first lady is also pressured to present herself, both physically and attitudinally, in a manner considered appropriate for her elevated social stature.

Being the national hostess is one of the most historically entrenched expectations placed on the president's spouse. When Martha Washington joined her husband in New York (then the nation's capital), she was forbidden from accepting invitations for private dinners at people's homes, so she carved out a social niche for herself by hosting her own social events. Her receptions and teas were initially small but cordial gatherings for which she planned guest lists, ordered refreshments, and guided topics of conversation. After the capital was relocated to Philadelphia, Washington reportedly began hosting more lavish balls, galas, and formal dinners. As the initial first lady, Martha Washington established the president's mate as the national hostess, and most subsequent first ladies followed suit.

For the wives of the early presidents, the affairs they organized offered an opportunity to participate in the political system at a time when women were disenfranchised. Through what might be considered a sort of dinner party diplomacy, they helped forward their husbands' agendas, shared their own opinions on issues of the day, and asserted what power they could within the constraints of existing social mores and political structures. As women have become more empowered, the party-giver role for the presidential spouse has changed but not disappeared. Both Michelle Obama and Melania Trump have served as the national hostess for a wide range of activities, from family-friendly gatherings like the White House Easter Egg Roll to traditional teas and receptions as well as highly formal state dinners. In each case, the women have been judged for their ability to adapt to the situation while maintaining a sense of grace and elegance befitting the first lady.

Michelle Obama began participating in the customary ceremonial engagements of the first lady as soon as she moved into the White House. She welcomed local children to an event celebrating Black History month in February, invited families to help cultivate a new White House garden in the spring, hosted the largest-ever crowd for the traditional Easter Egg Roll in April, and held a jazz concert in early summer to kick off the White House music series. She entertained the spouses of world leaders during the G-20 economic summit in the fall, and organized various receptions and teas throughout the year. Whether due to her selection of White House holiday décor or her demeanor as she gave tours to reporters, Obama was frequently commended for her amiability and her sense of discernment. Her guest lists included people from different backgrounds and earned her a great deal of positive media coverage. She was also regularly praised for her looks and was applauded for assuming a conventional approach to the first ladyship without letting her identity be subsumed by her husband.

Obama's ceremonial duties were more expansive than those of many early first ladies and reflected the broad range of rituals contemporary presidential mates take part in. Within months of acquiring her new position, Obama fielded many invitations to be a commencement speaker at high schools and colleges across the country, something Barbara Bush and Hillary Clinton both did. She also began acting as a goodwill ambassador, much like Jacqueline Kennedy and Pat Nixon, while touring various parts of Europe and Asia with the president. Obama was occasionally critiqued for a minor misstep in protocol or a seeming overindulgence (such as privately employing a makeup artist for her tour of Europe), but she was most often touted as an admirable representative of American womanhood.

Melania Trump's decision to postpone moving into the White House meant the first lady's national hostess activities were less prominent than those of her predecessor. As she had promised during the transition period, she did fly from New York to DC in order to attend many traditional ceremonies during the early months of her first ladyship. Trump was present to greet several foreign dignitaries and their wives. She also hosted a number of teas and receptions, such as her March luncheon to celebrate International Women's Day and her May gathering for military mothers, but her engagements did not draw much media attention. Once Barron finished his school year and Melania joined Donald in the White House full-time, her activity level rose considerably. Although Trump did not deliver any commencement addresses, she did accompany her husband as a goodwill ambassador overseas. Her late-spring trip included some criticism for an expensive Dolce & Gabbana jacket she wore in Italy, but her appearance throughout her travels was generally dubbed appropriate, ladylike, and stylish.

Trump reportedly consulted with the US State Department to assure that her wardrobe met the standards of protocol for each stop on the Trumps' overseas tour, but she conformed to the pressures of regional sartorial practices only on a selective basis. Her decision not to wear a headscarf during a visit to Saudi Arabia earned her praise and put her in the company of Michelle Obama, Theresa May, and Angela Merkel, none of whom put on a headscarf during their various trips to the Middle East. When she did don a veil for a meeting with the pope, however, commentators applauded Trump for deferring to local norms and for showing respect to the pontiff.

The most prominent example of the modern first lady functioning as the national hostess occurs when she plans and executes a state dinner. The formal meal is a tradition that began when Julia and Ulysses Grant hosted the Hawaiian King David Kalakaua in 1874. Julia left the seating arrangements and wine selection to Ulysses, but she set a precedent for the first ladies who succeeded her by managing all other aspects of the evening. Formal state dinners became fairly regular events after the 1874 affair. At the turn of the twentieth century, the White House was remodeled, and the State Dining Room was added. Dinners for foreign heads of state are customarily held in this designated space that seats approximately 150 guests. The planning of a state dinner is now considered a primary responsibility of the president's spouse and the Office of the First Lady.[1] The matriarch of the White House sets the theme, chooses the menu, selects the place settings, and makes all of the requisite arrangements for what are usually the most elegant gatherings an administration holds.

Because the first lady is in charge of planning it, each state dinner offers the opportunity for the White House matron to impact the ways the American public, world leaders, and people from the honored guest's nation perceive her. Most state dinners are formal affairs that include a multicourse meal, entertainment of various sorts, and toasts and comments from key attendees. Still an example of dinner party diplomacy, the occasion offers an interesting blend of political and social interactions intended to strengthen ties between the nations and their leaders. First ladies have been both praised and chastised for their state dinners. Eleanor Roosevelt broke with many traditions when she hosted King George VI of England at the Roosevelts' Hyde Park home for what was described as an American cookout. Pundits were initially appalled that she served the monarch hot dogs and hamburgers in a casual setting. When the British king complimented the meal, attitudes turned, and Roosevelt was applauded for promoting an American tradition. Aside from a few such notable exceptions, the state dinner has been a black (or sometimes white) tie event held at the White House.

Michelle Obama gave her first state dinner on November 24, 2009. The guest of honor was the prime minister of India Manmohan Singh. Obama had earned a reputation for having good taste but had not yet hosted the grandest of White House functions, so the press and public were eager to see what she would do. When it was announced that the dinner would be served on the south lawn, concerns began to grow about Obama's decision-making. The Indian media admonished the first lady and questioned her selection of a tent for the location; some even claimed it was an incredible show of disrespect. Members of the American press also criticized the choice of location and used Nancy Reagan's 1988 Rose Garden dinner for the president of Turkey, Kenan Evren, to explain the problems an outdoor gathering created. Pundits wondered if the self-professed "girl from the south side of Chicago" possessed the refinement necessary to arrange a state dinner.

Obama evidently chose a south lawn tent for her first state dinner because of her extensive guest list. The dinner for the prime minister included over four hundred dignitaries, celebrities, Washington insiders, media figures, and other friends and acquaintances. It was one of the largest and most lavish dinners held for any foreign head of state. To adorn the tables with enough place settings, Obama chose a blend of past presidential china sets from the Eisenhower, Clinton, and George W. Bush administrations. The threat of rain forced the welcoming reception indoors, but the bulk of the evening was a success. The tent was decorated with a variety of lights and flowers that gave it a "less stately, more romantic"[2] feel than the State Dining Room. Guests dressed in both American- and Indian-inspired attire, so the room was filled with a mix of vibrant colored saris, basic black dresses, and assorted tuxedos. Michelle Obama wore a silver embroidered strapless gown made by an Indian-born designer and accessorized with traditional Indian churis. The mostly vegetarian dinner was a nod to the guest of honor. It included items grown in Obama's White House garden and won wide approval by many food critics. After dinner the National Symphony Orchestra, Bay Area Empire Bhangra dancers, and Chicago-based jazz musicians performed for the crowd.

The execution of Obama's first state dinner quelled concerns about her skills as a hostess. Food and wine reviewers, fashion commentators, and politicos all praised the first lady. The foreign press commended Obama's thoughtfulness and acknowledged the many references to Indian culture she incorporated into the evening. Still, not all responses were positive. Some observers contended that the banquet was too showy, calling it more evocative of a Hollywood gala than a serious political affair and claiming it reflected Michelle Obama's desire to be a celebrity rather than a public servant. A few political analysts complained that the cost of the evening was not commensurate with the diplomatic gains it garnered. Conservative writers pointed to Laura Bush's more understated and conventional approach to such dinners as a way of subtly berating Obama's bold style. Perhaps the most biting critique involved charges that the opulent gathering was inappropriate in light of the economic struggles average Americans were facing at the time; some pundits argued Obama's extravagant bash called into question the sincerity of her professed concern for ordinary citizens.

On April 24, 2018, Melania Trump hosted her first state dinner when she and her husband welcomed the president of France, Emmanuel Macron, and his wife, Brigitte, to the White House. There was some initial trepidation regarding Trump's ability to pull together the affair. However, unlike the 2009 concerns that Obama lacked the sophistication necessary to do the job, worries about Trump revolved around whether she would embrace this particular duty of a president's mate or simply let her husband run the show. Such apprehensions were eased when the Office of the First Lady informed members of the press that Mrs. Trump had been studying past state dinners and the protocols surrounding them. When it came time to plan the night, Trump declined the help of outside consultants and directly took charge. She was said to have selected every element of the evening "from the entrée to the chair cushions"[3] with no input from the president.

Trump's first state dinner was a very traditional affair reminiscent of many past gatherings. The banquet was held in the State Dining Room and had a smaller guest list than most of Michelle Obama's and many of Laura Bush's dinners. While spokespeople for the Trump administration claimed the smaller set of invitees was because Melania wanted to make the evening a more intimate and engaging experience, many pundits speculated that it was actually a reflection of the president's inability to attract the kind of star power the Obamas had. Trump used china sets from the Clinton and George W. Bush administrations and developed a cream-and-gold color scheme for the décor. She used white sweet peas and cherry blossoms in the floral arrangements. In deference to her guests and her own past as a model in Paris, Trump's dress was haute couture from Chanel. A shimmering, hand-painted Chantilly lace piece with silver sequins and beading, the gown was adapted from a jumpsuit Chanel creative director Karl Lagerfeld said reflected his own positive feelings about President Macron.[4] Trump's menu highlighted French influences on American cooking. She served a goat cheese gateau and tomato jam with buttermilk biscuit crumbles and baby lettuces to start.

The entrée was a rack of spring lamb drizzled with a French onion, butter, and cream sauce and a side of Cajun-spiced gold rice jambalaya. For dessert, guests enjoyed a nectarine tart with crème fraîche. The crowd was treated to a performance by the Washington National Opera.

Melania Trump's inaugural state dinner was heavily influenced by many of her predecessors. The use of cherry blossoms in the floral arrangements referenced Helen "Nellie" Taft, who pushed for planting the trees (a gift from Japan) in DC as part of a city beautification project. Trump's choice of small circular tables recalled Jackie Kennedy's preferred seating arrangement. The use of Clinton and Bush place settings added nods to Hillary and Laura. In addition, many of the herbs used in the dinner were from the White House garden, and the honey for the dessert came from the White House beehive, both structures developed by Michelle Obama.

By most accounts, Melania Trump's first state dinner was a stunning success. She was said to have embodied the first ladyship more completely and comfortably while planning and executing the grand event than she had at any other point during her time in the White House. Many commentators claimed the dinner put her unique skill sets on display and gave her the opportunity to fulfill the classic responsibilities of a presidential spouse. She was described as elegant, graceful, thoughtful, and hospitable. For many pundits, Trump was the ideal national hostess because she demonstrated her ability to manage a large-scale social function; underscored her deftness at negotiating the domestic elements of the White House; looked impeccable; and garnered positive media attention without overshadowing her husband, her guests, or the diplomatic elements of the occasion.

During their initial state dinners, Michelle Obama and Melania Trump both showed deference to their guests of honor in their construction of the menu, their chosen attire, and their adherence to protocol. They each created exquisite environments that were a tribute to the situation and its historical relevance while also including unique displays of the host's own tastes and personality. Obama's bold choices reflected her intrepid style, whereas Trump's more traditional dinner bolstered her efforts to be a conventional first lady.

PUBLIC SOCIAL ADVOCATE*

In spite of the fact that most presidents' wives find the attention paid them troubling in many ways, most also discover that they can parlay such notice into a form of rhetorical power (sometimes called the "first lady pulpit") that helps them champion causes they particularly value. Although originally less well publicized than the galas and receptions they hosted, social advocacy has been a key part of the first lady's job since the founding of the republic. Martha Washington used her own money and fame to aid Revolutionary War veterans, Abigail Adams was a proponent of women's rights, Louisa Adams argued for the abolition of slavery, Mary Todd Lincoln supported organizations that helped freed slaves become educated and employed, Ida McKinley helped raise funds for widows and orphans of military personnel, and Nellie Taft successfully lobbied for legislation regarding health and safety standards in the workplace.

Some twentieth-century wives focused their time and efforts on what might be considered apolitical feminine issues, such as Jackie Kennedy's arts initiatives and Lady Bird Johnson's highway beautification program, but many other savvy presidential spouses utilized their power to improve the lives of citizens in different ways. Betty Ford reduced the social stigma surrounding alcoholism, Nancy Reagan urged Americans to "Just Say No" to drugs, and Barbara Bush promoted literacy. Rosalynn Carter and Hillary Clinton each tried to directly impact legislation related to mental and physical health care but were criticized for stepping outside the equivocal boundaries of their role. Carter and Clinton serve as reminders that the rhetorical power of the first lady pulpit does have limits.

Most East Wing activism relies on the first lady's ability to draw attention to particular issues. The use of the first lady pulpit has expanded considerably as communication technologies have evolved and made it easier for presidential spouses to directly appeal to the public. For

---

* Presidents' spouses can and do effect change privately, but the focus here is on their public activities.

contemporary first ladies, the capacity to reach a broader audience gives them more influence but also creates pressure for them to develop clear and actionable initiatives. The selection of specific causes is guided by the individual woman's personal interests, the prominent social issues of the time period, and a desire to enhance the first lady's public image by underscoring her compassion for others. Most recent presidential consorts have chosen familiar kid- and family-oriented projects. Both Michelle Obama and Melania Trump addressed subjects related to improving the well-being of children. In addition, Obama became a prominent supporter of military families.

Michelle Obama's agenda was fairly expansive. Because of the challenging economic environment at the outset of her husband's first term, she spent quite a bit of time touring homeless shelters, visiting education and job placement centers, and encouraging volunteerism as a form of employment preparedness. However, the specific initiatives she championed that are most explicitly tied to her are the *Let's Move!* campaign she initiated for children and her multiple programs (cosponsored by Jill Biden, the vice president's wife) to aid military families. During her second term as first lady, Obama also sponsored *Let Girls Learn*, an international effort to improve females' access to education. All of her major efforts shared a particular focus on children, demonstrating the sincerity of her 2008 election claim that "all our children's future is my stake in this election"[5] and helping solidify her standing as the nation's "mom-in-chief."

Let's Move! was Obama's longest lasting and most prominent campaign. It was a healthy lifestyle crusade that encouraged children to develop beneficial habits they could maintain throughout their lives. The program drew attention to the problem of childhood obesity, touted the benefits of exercise, and promoted eating a wholesome diet. The project was developed and implemented rather quickly; just two months after moving into the White House, as part of the initiative, Obama invited schoolchildren to the grounds to help plant what became known as the White House Kitchen Garden.[6] Throughout the campaign, Obama elicited help from sports figures and celebrities to create videos about exercise and combined forces with people from the National Football League's *Play 60* program that urges kids to engage in physical play for sixty minutes every day. Obama went on numerous entertainment programs, including daytime and late-night talk shows, to publicize her efforts. On these venues she talked about healthy food choices and demonstrated ways to make exercise fun—she even challenged hosts and other guests to on-screen dance competitions and push-up contests. Obama routinely blended lighthearted and upbeat activities with serious information about childhood obesity and its effects.

Obama's *Let's Move!* efforts also included a push to make school lunches more nutritious. She supported the Healthy, Hunger-Free Kids Act of 2010, a statute that mandated changes to federally funded school lunch programs that provide free and reduced-cost lunches to children from low-income families. The intent was to help school cafeterias manage serving sizes, reduce sodium content in the food, and increase the number of fruits and vegetables offered so that even disadvantaged students could eat better. Obama and her staff pressed for changes to school lunch content, provided information that justified legislative intervention, and presented specific recommendations that became part of the regulations that were eventually issued.

Even though Obama's program seemed relatively noncontroversial, it still sparked a great deal of criticism. Particular objections took different forms, but many critiques of *Let's Move!* stemmed from concerns that Obama was degrading the first ladyship. Some writers claimed that Obama's appearances in workout wear were not appropriate for someone of her social rank. They also decried her willingness to get on the ground to do push-ups in public and protested that her dance style (when promoting dance as a form of exercise) was undignified. Some pundits also asserted that Obama sought too much attention for herself and was just trying to cultivate her own celebrity status. Critics denounced such self-promotion as unladylike.

More pointed protests about the first lady's *Let's Move!* campaign revolved around the notion that she had overstepped the boundaries of her position by impacting federal legislation. Like other first ladies who tried to spur concrete government action, Obama was chided for moving beyond the first lady pulpit and asserting power through other means. Journalists questioned the appropriateness of having a person who had not been elected or appointed wielding such influence—a query raised whenever a presidential spouse demonstrates her own political power. Such complaints presume that a president's mate should cease to act as an empowered citizen because of her husband's job. The most ardent critics described Obama as power-hungry and aggressive.

Other grievances about the first lady and her project disputed the sincerity of Obama's concern for children. Students across the country protested the new lunch standards; they used a social media campaign to complain about the smaller portions, claim the food tasted bad, and show that the undesired fruits and vegetables were going to waste. Turning the idea of a national mother figure into something of an evil caricature, pockets of students, parents, and reporters across the country painted Obama's efforts as those of an overprotective matriarch attempting to control the lives of everyone around her. Conservative commentators amplified this image by framing the first lady as the mastermind behind the creation of a so-called nanny state. Critics argued that Obama was trying to stifle American citizens' freedom by curtailing their right to choose to be unhealthy. The protests did negatively impact some perceptions of Michelle Obama, but her overall popularity remained relatively high throughout her time in the White House.

Melania Trump took considerably longer to announce her East Wing agenda after becoming the first lady than her predecessor did. Although she engaged in some of the same advocacy activities (e.g., visiting hospitals, schools, and charity organizations) as past first ladies, her delayed move to the White House meant she was slower than many when it came to identifying her signature cause. During the campaign, Trump made generic claims about working to improve the lives of children and identified cyberbullying as a key issue she would like to address, but she spent over a year trying to shape her interests into a concrete agenda. When she did present her official social advocacy campaign, the project spanned many elements that Trump argued adversely impacted children and families.

On May 7, 2018, fifteen months after becoming the first lady of the United States, Trump held a press conference to unveil her *Be Best* campaign. The multifaceted initiative revolved around children and spanned several topics but had three guiding themes: general well-being, social media use, and opioid abuse.[7] Each pillar of the program contained additional, slightly more specific topics of concern. As part of her efforts to improve children's well-being, Trump promoted healthy living, kindness, general encouragement, and respect. Under the umbrella of social media use, Trump urged parents and other adults to teach children how to express themselves respectfully and compassionately online. The opioid abuse element focused particularly on supporting families affected by drug addiction and drawing attention to pregnancy-related problems stemming from the misuse of pain medication.

For the most part, *Be Best* appeared to be less action-oriented than *Let's Move!* It emphasized coaxing others to have conversations with children about the issues young people confront. The initial rollout of the campaign offered some advice regarding talking to children about their online activities and recognized specific individuals who were already helping others improve their sense of comfort and belonging. The *Be Best* page on the White House website contained a few short videos and a slew of photographs of the first lady interacting with children and hosting meetings about technology and drug addiction, but the site offered little actionable information. Despite the fact that the issues mentioned in the *Be Best* launch were timely, important, and within the realm of purportedly appropriate concerns for a first lady, the campaign inspired several critiques.

The first complaint about *Be Best* was its name. Unlike Nancy Reagan's directive *Just Say No* (to drugs) or Michelle Obama's inclusive invitation *Let's Move!*, Trump's *Be Best* title was awkward and grammatically confusing. This led to widespread haranguing of the first lady and her staff for their inability to construct a simple message. Some sympathetic commentators excused the title by attributing its awkwardness to the fact that Trump is not a native English speaker. Less kind reporters mocked the error and linked Trump's poor messaging to her husband's tendency to speak and write incoherently; after the *Be Best* press conference, some writers called Melania a true reflection of Donald's anti-intellectual disposition. The irksome name gave critics an opportunity to cast aspersions on the foreign first lady's mental capacities and to stereotype her based on her thick accent. The phrase "Be Best" became fodder for comedic monologues on late-night television shows, prompting one prominent host to scold the first lady's staff for not correcting the mistake and to prod members of the Office of the First Lady to "be better."[8]

In addition to its problematic slogan, the *Be Best* campaign was also faulted for its lack of structure. After taking so long to announce her signature initiative, the relative vagueness of Trump's program was surprising. Some journalists described the project as a set of platitudes designed to make the first lady appear caring and concerned without her having to actually do anything. Others claimed the *Be Best* website was simply a public relations effort to draw attention to the various events Trump had already participated in. The lack of specificity, coupled with Trump's explanation that the initiative was intended to support existing programs rather than create new ones, reignited concerns about Trump's desire to serve as an active, competent, and engaged first lady.

Many discussions about the elements of Trump's *Be Best* campaign brought up recurring attacks that had plagued Melania Trump throughout her time as a candidate's spouse, the wife of the president-elect, and the first lady, but perhaps the most bothersome one grew out of comparisons between Trump and Michelle Obama. Trying to explain the faulty title, reporters tied Trump's phrase to a comment Obama had made about sexism in the workplace. Journalists argued Trump took Obama's response to a question about what men can do to discourage sexism ("Be better," she said) and recycled it in an incorrect and amplified manner. Whether true or not, the story gained traction and was repeated in many online and mainstream media sources. Moreover, the one bit of actionable information provided by the first lady at the *Be Best* launch was said to have also been taken from Michelle Obama. A link from the campaign website led to an online pamphlet by the Federal Trade Commission titled "Talking with Kids About Being Online." The FTC document was almost identical to one created during the Obama era. In spite of the fact that there was no evidence that Michelle Obama authored the original pamphlet, people across social media and members of the press were quick to accuse Trump of once again plagiarizing materials from her predecessor. The assertions fortified the idea that Trump was unwilling or unable to develop her own interests or activities.

Both Michelle Obama and Melania Trump followed in the tradition of their forerunners by being public social advocates. They each chose to focus on improving the lives of children but did so in markedly different ways. Obama was very active and visible, creating programs that involved young people in healthful living experiences (such as helping plant and harvest the White House Kitchen Garden), promoting and participating in events that demonstrated diverse approaches to fitness, and pressing for legislation that enhanced children's access to nutritious foods. She sometimes partnered with others who were undertaking similar work, but she also developed and distributed unique messages of her own. Trump's long-awaited program was less hands-on and was designed to draw attention to existing initiatives executed by others. Her statement of support for people and organizations already tackling large social issues was a means of lending the power of the first lady pulpit to those she deemed worthy of endorsement.

The approaches Obama and Trump took earned the women some praise and quite a bit of criticism. They were commended for their decisions to focus on the plight of children, a common priority among past first ladies, yet their specific efforts inspired questions regarding each woman's ability to serve as first lady. Obama's activity produced objections about her alleged pursuit of power and aspersions that she was not sufficiently demure. Trump's more hands-off approach spurred complaints about her lack of interest in being a presidential helpmate and in laboring on behalf of her fellow citizens; she was reprimanded for leaving the hard work of social leadership to others.

FIGURE OF COMPASSION

In addition to serving as the national hostess and as a champion of particular causes, the first lady is also expected to be the compassionate face of the presidential administration. When national tragedies occur, the public looks first to the president for a response and then often turns to the president's wife as a potential source of sympathy, sensitivity, and kindness to those in need. The character of the event varies and can include external threats such as the terrorist attacks of September 11, 2001; natural disasters like hurricanes, floods, and earthquakes; or domestic troubles like bombings and mass shootings. Other crises are politically inspired, like wars, international conflicts, and other administrative actions. Whatever the situation, modern first ladies are expected to provide messages offering an appropriate blend of consolation, empathy, and support whenever a national calamity occurs.

Presidential spouses have long provided solace to the nation. Rooted in presumed female attributes related to nurturing and caring for others, when challenging times have arisen, first ladies have historically become the "consolers-in-chief." As wartime first ladies, Edith Wilson and Eleanor Roosevelt offered messages of hope to military families and helped citizens combat feelings of helplessness by urging people to join the war effort through participating in conservation plans like going meatless on Mondays and planting Victory Gardens. They also encouraged people to collect and recycle rubber, metal, and other essential materials. The women participated too, becoming role models who gave comfort to their worried countrymen.

In a more personal example of a first lady helping to console the nation, Jacqueline Kennedy's behavior in the aftermath of her husband's assassination made the grieving widow an iconic representation of grace in a time of tragedy. Her apparently calm presence at the hastily arranged swearing-in of Lyndon Johnson provided equanimity to the transfer of power in spite of the devastating reason for the shift in leadership. Although she did not give any speeches in the days after her husband's death and receded from public view for some time after John's funeral, Kennedy's demeanor during the hours after JFK's death and her composure throughout the public events surrounding his entombment offered a stunned nation a model for mourning with dignity.

Contemporary first ladies have, by virtue of improved communication technologies, been forced into quicker and more active responses to national crises than their predecessors. Whereas Nellie Taft did not send condolences regarding the sinking of the Titanic until weeks after the tragedy, Barbara Bush expressed compassion for victims of Hurricane Andrew (a storm that destroyed much of the US Gulf Coast in August 1992) almost immediately and visited the affected areas as soon as it was deemed safe to do so. She toured the region alongside her husband and demonstrated concern for displaced families. Bush visited storm survivors and distributed battery-operated radios so those without power could stay informed about the situation. She showed sympathy

for victims through television and radio interviews and urged people
outside of the impact zone to send donations.

In April 1995, an act of domestic terrorism shook the nation when
three former members of the military bombed a federal building in
Oklahoma City, killing over 165 people and injuring at least 680 others.
Three days later, First Lady Hillary Clinton took over her husband's
weekly radio address to send a message of comfort specifically to the
nation's children. In it, she acknowledged their fear and confusion and
reminded her audience that the number of good people in the world
far exceeds the number of evil ones. She encouraged listeners to think
about the kindness of others and to consider the various types of positive actions each of them could get involved in to help make the world
a better place. Clinton's brief comments reflected the content of many
recent first ladies' post-tragedy messages; they conveyed sympathy and
concern for victims, commended the work of first responders, reminded
the audience of the kindness and goodness in the world, and prompted
constructive reactions by citizens.

Laura Bush carried a particularly heavy burden consoling the nation
as the first lady. Just shy of nine months into her husband's first term in
office there was a massive foreign terrorist attack on US soil. The historic
and tragic September 11 events urged the heretofore relatively quiet Bush
to use the first lady pulpit to remember the dead, show concern for the
injured, and convey regard for first responders. Many journalists and
scholars argue that, after the tragedy, Bush found her political voice as
a national maternal figure who helped comfort a shocked and wounded
country. As the military pursuit of the organizers of the assault ensued,
Bush embodied compassionate patriotism as she supported her husband's actions and indicated her concern and gratitude for the families
of deployed armed forces personnel. Then, in August 2005, Bush found
herself in a similar situation as her mother-in-law had thirteen years
earlier when a powerful hurricane pummeled the Gulf Coast. After Hurricane Katrina struck, there were serious criticisms about the president's
handling of the crisis, and Bush was left trying to console a public that
was not only distressed but angry too. She made visits to the affected
area, expressed condolences for the almost two thousand people who
died in the storm and its aftermath, and encouraged action on behalf of

thousands of displaced citizens. Her sincerity was never questioned, but many people denounced her inability to pressure her husband to more effectively respond to the catastrophe.

Both Michelle Obama and Melania Trump had to comfort a wounded nation during various crises. Like many other first ladies, Michelle Obama and Melania Trump were called upon to comment on devastating natural disasters. Obama sent messages of support for victims and praise for first responders after forest fires ravaged parts of the western United States, when floodwaters soaked the Midwest, and when tornadoes leveled homes in numerous different states. In 2012, just days before her husband was elected for a second term in office, Hurricane Sandy swept along the eastern seaboard, wreaking havoc in several states and crippling New Jersey and parts of New York. Michelle Obama was on the campaign trail when the storm hit and reassured crowds that Barack's priority was helping storm victims. She used social media and mainstream news outlets to send messages of gratitude to first responders, call for unity in support of victims, and offer prayers for all who were affected. In addition, she orchestrated donation collections and maintained a hopeful tone about the speed of cleanup efforts. A few days after the storm surges subsided, she visited parts of New Jersey impacted by the storm and met with children to comfort them and show concern for their well-being. Obama's response to Hurricane Sandy was widely applauded.

In the fall of the first year of the Trump presidency, an atypically active hurricane season caused massive destruction across many parts of the United States and its territories. Three named hurricanes (Harvey, Irma, and Maria) hit Florida, the Gulf Coast, and Puerto Rico, respectively, causing extensive loss of life and damage to homes, schools, businesses, and hospitals. Melania Trump almost immediately posted messages of support through social media, sharing thoughts and prayers for people in the affected areas. In mid-October, Trump visited many sites impacted by the three storms and helped serve boxed lunches to victims. She also created a public service announcement that encouraged others to donate whatever they could to help people in need of assistance. Trump was commended for her efforts, earning praise for her active involvement in relief efforts. She was initially chastised for wearing high-heeled shoes as she departed the White House for her tour of the afflicted areas, but she was subsequently complimented for her attire on the ground; she wore jeans and a baseball cap while in the storm-ravaged regions—a move many commentators saw as an improvement over some of her predecessors, who appeared less comfortable as they interacted with struggling citizens while wearing dresses, pantsuits, and, in some cases, pearls. Although her response to the hurricanes was viewed as effective, Trump suffered a problem like the one Laura Bush confronted after Hurricane Katrina. When Trump's husband received harsh criticism for failing to provide sufficient aid to specific areas, many pundits, journalists, and members of the public began to question the value of Melania's proffered thoughts and prayers in the face of her husband's inactivity.

One type of tragedy that both Michelle Obama and Melania Trump had to regularly comment on that most of their forebears did not was mass shootings. During the eight years Obama was in the White House, nine incidents occurred during which someone wielding a gun killed ten or more individuals. Within the first eighteen months of Trump's tenure as first lady, five such catastrophes happened. The massacres took place in locales as diverse as schools, military bases, nightclubs, churches, movie theaters, and workplaces. There were five mass shootings during Nancy Reagan's eight years in the White House, but most other modern first ladies suffered two or fewer on their watch.

Michelle Obama's responses to mass shootings were in some ways similar to those for natural disasters. She made initial comments consoling survivors and praising first responders, and then she met with people affected, like the parents of the elementary school children killed at Sandy Hook and patrons of the *Pulse* nightclub in Orlando. After such shootings Obama openly condemned the violent acts and those who perpetrated them. She also called for legislation mandating enhanced gun control. As the number of shootings increased, her statements about the need for government action to limit access to certain types of guns became more specific and more pointed. She advocated for more extensive background checks for gun purchasers and mental health screenings for buyers. Her messaging regarding gun control was couched in terms of showing compassion for the victims, trying to prevent further tragedies, and having a regard for the safety and well-being of America's children. Even though her display of concern was welcomed, her support for legislation earned Obama a great deal of pushback from people who argued she was politicizing the devastating events in order to undermine the Second Amendment of the US Constitution. Because gun control is a highly divisive topic, Obama's efforts to console the nation's citizens were viewed by some as creating schisms among Americans rather than unifying the nation.

Melania Trump's messages regarding mass shootings were also consistent with her responses to natural disasters. Her initial comments included sending thoughts and prayers. Like Obama, some of Trump's first comments were disseminated on social media sites like Twitter and were quickly followed by audio or video comments on official White House websites or through the mainstream press. Trump also sometimes met with survivors or families of those killed in the attacks. The first such tragedy to happen during Trump's time in the White House occurred on October 1, 2017, when a gunman opened fire on concertgoers in Las Vegas. The morning after the incident, Trump tweeted "My heart and prayers goes [sic] out to victims, families & loved ones! #PrayForLasVegas."[9] Later that day, Trump joined her husband on the White House lawn for a moment of silence in remembrance of those killed, and two days later she accompanied her husband to a Las Vegas hospital to meet with people injured in the assault. Trump expressed an interest in donating blood while at the hospital, but she was not allowed to do so due to presidential security guidelines and because her donation would not meet FDA guidelines (The FDA has indefinitely deferred donations from people who lived in Europe between 1980 and 1996 in an effort to prevent the spread of mad cow disease among humans). Trump's reactions to other mass shootings were similar, though she did not always visit the affected areas but instead invited groups (like the students from Parkland, Florida) to the White House.

Melania Trump's responses to the mass shootings that occurred during her first several months in the White House were active and compassionate but measured. Unlike Obama, who called for stricter gun laws in the wake of such tragedies, Trump never directly discussed government intervention. The fact that her husband was a pro-gun Republican who made protection of the Second Amendment a major theme of his 2016 campaign rendered it difficult for her to plead for legislative action. However, the first lady did argue in favor of giving student protesters fighting for gun control a voice and said she was heartened by their willingness to join in the debate about their future. Even though she did not actually state a position regarding the regulation of firearms, commentators and journalists amplified her support for the Parkland students. Some pundits lauded Trump for expressing an opinion that contradicted her husband's public stance but complained that her own statements about feeling powerless weakened her encouragement of the students. Others tried to invalidate her perspective by claiming she had no credibility or right to speak on the subject of gun control.

Melania Trump found herself in an unusual situation relative to addressing crises during her second year in the White House when she was pressured to address a political and humanitarian calamity brought about by the actions of her husband and members of his administration. In May and June 2018, the Department of Justice initiated a zero-tolerance policy regarding people crossing into the United States without proper documentation. The US government began jailing illegal border crossers and separating accompanying children from the offenders. Within a few weeks, reports surfaced that border patrol agents had divided numerous families and that over two thousand children of various ages had been locked away in makeshift detention facilities across the southwestern United States. Groups of citizens around the nation protested the separations, and the United Nations condemned the policy as a human rights violation. Many members of the press and the public began calling on Melania Trump to speak out against her husband, some pointing to her history as an immigrant, others to her standing as a mother, and still others to her professed interest in protecting kids as reasons she should act on behalf of the captive children.

By June 19, all living former first ladies had publicly denounced the president, his administration, and his party for engaging in what each variously characterized as callous and un-American behavior. Reports began emerging that Trump was pushing her husband to change his policy, and the president later credited her with his modest change of heart. On June 21, Melania boarded a plane to visit some of the children's holding facilities in person. Although a scandal ensued regarding her choice of clothing for the trip, her presence helped mute some criticisms about the first lady's purported inactivity. She made a second visit about a week later with the stated intent of improving living conditions for the children and monitoring their safety. (For more details regarding this scandal and Trump's response to it, see chapter 4.)

Trump's efforts to address the politically induced tragedy of family separations at the border were important for a variety of reasons. They underscored the sincerity of her concern for children and demonstrated her ability to function as an individual political entity. Her willingness to assert private and public influence over her husband also helped to shift the prevailing narrative that she had no interest in being the first lady. In addition, she navigated a type of crisis communication for which there were very few templates to follow.

While trying to respond to national crises, Michelle Obama and Melania Trump experienced the double-edged sword of being a first lady— they were required to speak but expected to limit their comments. To do otherwise meant facing disapproval for stepping outside the ambiguous boundaries of the position. Even framing their perspectives in terms of concern for children did not always give them much space to maneuver. Each woman had to find her own voice when consoling the nation and acting as a model of kindness and support during difficult times.

Even though the first lady has no codified job description, there are at least a few common requirements someone in that position must fulfill. Presidents' wives are expected to serve as the national hostess, be a social advocate, and act as the compassionate face of the administration. As demonstrated above, however, completing these duties can be tricky for any first lady. Michelle Obama and Melania Trump at times received praise for their actions, but they were also regularly berated for how they managed their responsibilities.

FASHION ICON

From news reports about the arrival of Martha Washington in New York that provided detailed information about her travel attire to critiques of Melania Trump's footwear during an event in the White House garden, and from the collection of inaugural ball gowns in the Smithsonian to the queries about who paid for Michelle Obama's wardrobe, the public has long been preoccupied with the first lady's clothing. The widespread obsession with the presidential mate's look has ranged from assessing how ladylike she seems to deciphering hidden messages she is supposedly sending with her attire.

The amount of consideration given to the sartorial presentation of the president's wife sometimes becomes overwhelming and the focus on her appearance can create lasting, but not always positive, impressions. Jackie Kennedy's clothing became such a dominant part of the legacy of her first ladyship that it regularly receives more attention than the many other contributions she made while in the White House. Rosalynn Carter was taunted for routinely wearing what some journalists called her "first lady uniform" of a modest A-line skirt, tucked-in blouse, and thin belt. Reports about the cost of Nancy Reagan's outfits portrayed her as a spoiled Hollywood star with no regard for the economic struggles of average Americans. Hillary Clinton's shoulder-padded suits became a trademark look and inspired digs about being too assertive and masculine that dogged her throughout her own political career.

Michelle Obama encountered some style-related issues that none of her predecessors confronted because of the different aspects of her identity. As a purported "everymom" figure, Obama was expected to reflect a relatable image that average American women could emulate. As the first African American first lady, people looked to Obama to represent her race. As a well-educated woman with a professional pedigree, she needed to reflect a sense of discernment. Of course, as the first lady, she had to engage in displays of conventional femininity that included an appropriate blend of elegance, approachability, and dignified self-presentation. Throughout her time in the White House, Obama met these separate but related expectations with varying degrees of success. Her wardrobe ranged from luxurious custom gowns to inexpensive T-shirts and shorts. She wore original pieces by famous designers and off-the-rack items from stores like J. Crew. Her expansive color palette included bright, bold hues and subtle, understated tones. She was rarely accused of being inappropriately attired and was often praised for being fashion-forward and for breaking the sartorial pattern of structured suits and dresses established by her immediate predecessors. Her flexible style enhanced her image with many citizens, but it also gave critics grounds for complaint.

Some objections to Obama's clothing choices were trivial comments about particular outfits. Fashion designers opposed Obama wearing a cardigan sweater over her sleeveless sundress for a meeting with Queen Elizabeth in 2009, and conservative pundits argued that her decision to wear a white dress with a black splatter print to tour the Gulf Coast after a massive oil spill in 2010 made it look like she was mocking the crisis. In 2015, the first lady received a mix of approbation and scorn, divided pretty solidly along partisan lines, when she decided to forgo the traditional headscarf when visiting Saudi Arabia. Minor grumblings about specific choices might have been irritating, but a larger set of sustained criticisms about Obama's looks were much more troubling.

Many persistent critiques regarding Michelle Obama's appearance were based on her unique physical attributes. Several conservative commentators disapproved of her bold color choices and argued that Obama's sleeveless dresses and tops were inappropriate for someone in her elevated social and political position. The complaints described her arms as strong, substantial, or muscular; talked about her broad shoulders; and included reminders of her supposedly unusual height and her dark skin tone. This species of labeling implied that the first lady possessed strikingly masculine characteristics and that she lacked the diminutive features of a "normal" presidential spouse. The fact that these not-so-subtle jabs at Obama ignored the numerous times Jackie Kennedy and others went sleeveless, the bright colors favored by women like Mamie Eisenhower and Nancy Reagan, and Barbara Bush's sturdy frame led some political analysts to condemn the racist undertones of the critiques. Because most of the same people who voiced objections about Obama's bare arms expressed no such concerns when Melania Trump went sleeveless, the claims of bias were rather convincing.

Melania Trump faced a different set of heightened expectations to be a fashionable first lady. As a former model and the proprietor of a line of cosmetics and accessories, there was a widespread assumption that the one thing Trump would excel at was being appropriately attired. The fact that the persona she cultivated for herself throughout the campaign was of a woman who was seen but never heard added to the pressure for her to express herself through her clothing. Furthermore, her stated intent to emulate women she considered traditional first ladies meant that her garments would likely include a mix of trendy looks with flattering but modest cuts. By most accounts, Trump took her attire seriously and many of her wardrobe choices helped enhance her public image. Her careful planning of every outfit for her first European tour as first lady indicated that she understood the importance of her outward image and that she cared about the messages it would send. However, like Obama, Trump's fashion choices were not always successful or conflict free.

Melania Trump's critics tended to search for reasons to rebuff the first lady for her appearance. She was berated for wearing high heels while departing the White House on a trip to visit hurricane survivors even though she changed her shoes before reaching the victims. Some politicos maintained she undermined her own charitable work when she wore Trump-licensed accessories while helping out at storm relief sites. One of the most common themes fueling protests about Trump's clothing involved cost. Reports about the first lady's activities routinely included information about the makeup of her outfit and the price of each item she wore. When she donned a $51,000 jacket at an economic summit in Italy in 2017, journalists and pundits harangued her for being out of touch with average Americans. (See chapter 4 for more on criticisms regarding Trump's expensive wardrobe.)

In addition to complaining about Trump's high-priced attire, the press and public often tried to decipher the presumed underlying meaning of many of her outfits. When she wore white to her husband's election night victory speech, some reporters said the one-shouldered jumpsuit was a respectful acknowledgment of her husband's opponent and others argued it was a snarky jab at the former first lady. Fourteen months later, when Melania arrived at Donald's first official State of the Union address wearing an all-white pantsuit, politicos again speculated about the implications of her garment. They debated whether the suit was an allusion to Clinton (an unconventional first lady), an acknowledgment of the suffragists, a sign of Trump's political awakening and empowerment, or simply a color she found flattering.

The game of interpreting Trump's sartorial expressions increased in intensity when she wore a thirty-nine-dollar, green, military-style coat on her trip to visit children separated from their parents at the southern US border. The jacket had the words "I REALLY DON'T CARE, DO U?" written across the back in large, graffiti-type white letters. Trump's outerwear and its significance became the dominant story of the news cycle for several days. Whereas the first lady's spokeswoman said that the article of clothing wasn't sending any message, the president contradicted her and claimed the lettering was a critique of what he called the "fake news" media. Other conservative commentators asserted that Melania Trump was pushing back at the press's tendency to make a big deal of her clothing. Some specifically stated that the first lady was trying to argue that people should not care about what she was wearing while she was on a mission of mercy. Less charitable assessments asserted that Trump was openly showing her lack of interest in being the presidential mate and that the jacket was more evidence that she was simply "going through the motions" of performing apparently mandatory tasks.

Michelle Obama and Melania Trump each had to confront the challenges of being one of the most visible women on the planet and a representative of American womanhood. As relatively young, fashionable presidential spouses, Obama and Trump carried weightier expectations than many of their predecessors when it came to being stylish. The women who came before them were required to be appropriately attired, but that mandate was relatively easy to fulfill when the women could develop a consistent, almost uniform-like manner of dress, like Rosalynn Carter, Barbara Bush, and Hillary Clinton had. For Obama and Trump, the early comparisons to Jacqueline Kennedy and the widespread social pressure placed on them to act as fashion icons were grounded in different elements of their personas but demanded they pay similar attention to their wardrobes. The ever-critical press and often-unforgiving public are eager to point out flaws in any first lady's appearance, but they were particularly keen on partisan-inspired attacks against Obama and Trump for various alleged sartorial infractions.

As the first lady of the land, the president's mate is a woman of high status traditionally likened in name and behavioral expectations to female members of the British monarchy. By frequently referring to Martha Washington, the very first spouse of a US president, as "Lady

Washington," the press and the public aligned the informal office she assumed with the royal hierarchy they had been accustomed to before the fight for independence. It wasn't until 1838 that the specific phrase "first lady" was applied to Washington and not until after 1849 that it became a common moniker for the mate of a president, but the idea that the spouse has important social standing and influence has guided many of the more consistent demands placed upon presidents' wives.

The job of first lady of the United States is odd. It comes with no clear list of duties but has seemingly ever-expanding requirements. Expectations for the president's mate have evolved over the years and have become so varied that although the first lady is not paid for her services, she is provided with a federally funded staff to help her. Despite some flexibility regarding the specific enactment of the role, the ability to mold the post to fit its inhabitant is limited; every woman who presides over the East Wing influences subsequent presidents' mates, and social mores of the era often dictate the parameters of acceptable behavior by a White House matriarch. Michelle Obama and Melania Trump each negotiated the historically stipulated tasks of the first lady in ways that variously conformed to and challenged established norms for the first lady functions of national hostess, public social advocate, model of compassion, and even fashion icon.

The two most recent first ladies each followed in the footsteps of others by actively participating in the rituals started by their predecessors. They hosted White House receptions, took part in ceremonial remembrances, and each even went to the funeral of a former first lady (Obama was present at Nancy Reagan's interment in 2016, and Trump attended Barbara Bush's in 2018). They each decorated the White House for Christmas and joined families on the south lawn for Easter festivities. The women acted as public advocates for social causes and as comforting figures in times of crisis. However, even though Obama and Trump did fulfill several expected functions, each did so in a manner that reflected her unique personality and distinguished her from her peers. Obama hosted state dinners, but made them memorable galas that included more participants and more daring color palettes than most previous such occasions. Trump confronted crises like her forebears had, but in order to serve as a compassionate voice on behalf of children she also purportedly pushed for a change in one of her husband's key political decisions. In addition, Obama and Trump had to negotiate changing communication expectations and exert the power of the first lady pulpit through social media.

As Michelle Obama and Melania Trump tried to forge their own paths as White House matron, they made numerous choices that influenced the ways they were perceived both in their own right and relative to the expectations of the position. Their actions, ranging from what clothes they wore to what causes they championed to what events they attended, became targets for attacks by the press and the public. The next chapter examines in more detail the ways both Michelle Obama and Melania Trump worked to surmount the criticisms they encountered and the controversies they endured.

FOUR

Can't Please Everyone

Managing Criticism and Scandal

FIRST LADIES ARE SUCH HIGHLY SCRUTINIZED FIGURES THAT NO president's mate has been able to escape all criticism during her time in the White House. From the clothes they wear, to the causes they champion, to the way they interact with their husbands or the citizenry, presidential spouses are always subject to protest—some facet of the public usually finds fault in the actions they take. Whether she is too demure or too bold, too active or too absent, too fashionable or too dowdy, it seems that no matron of the East Wing has ever been able to successfully represent all incarnations of the ideal American woman.

The long practice of judging the president's wife began when Martha Washington joined George after he assumed office. Washington received a mix of praise and condemnation upon her arrival in New York. Some reporters applauded her travel attire and noted that her clothing was manufactured in the United States, but others chided her expensive outfit and argued that her well-appointed coach was too reminiscent of the royal broughams in England. From the very beginning, the president's spouse was considered a public icon whose every action was open to potential derision by the press and the people. The difficult nature of the position was so evident from the start that, months before becoming the second woman to assume the role, Abigail Adams expressed reservations about being able to meet the expectations already placed on the consort of the US president.

All first ladies are ridiculed while residing in the White House. Some complaints are based on the personality of the individual married to the president, others stem from the amorphous expectations related to the role, and still others are a product of partisan gamesmanship. Attributes that are revered in some spouses are jeered in others, and no first lady's actions are so impeccable that she does not experience at least some degree of scorn. When a first lady engages in behavior that so clearly violates established norms that her reputation is adversely impacted, she might become entangled in a full-fledged scandal. The improprieties might be factual, such as Mary Todd Lincoln's misappropriation of federal funds and extortion of government appointees, or they could be based on rumor, as was Dolley Madison's purported affair with Thomas Jefferson. The alleged wrongdoing might involve the violation of federal law, like Florence Harding serving whiskey in the White House during Prohibition, or it could be a breach of social convention, as happened when Eleanor Roosevelt invited hundreds of African American guests to the White House—an action that today would be considered a positive break with established norms, but one that many found scandalous at the time.

One of the most prominent charges leveled against first ladies is overstepping the unclear boundaries of the role. Many women are accused of this type of misconduct while in the East Wing. The vast majority of such protestations are simple critiques of low-consequence activity, but sometimes the women's deportment invokes more concerted reproach. Perhaps the most serious example is the supposed misdeeds of Edith Wilson. After her husband, Woodrow, had a stroke, she became the gatekeeper to the president and assumed many of his duties instead of allowing the vice president to take over. Her actions were questioned at the time, but she nevertheless persisted in them for approximately seventeen months. Reporters and scholars later dubbed her the "first female president" as a way of both applauding her efforts and criticizing her unconstitutional assumption of power. Less overt but still controversial examples of first ladies ostensibly extending their political reach beyond the presumed limits of their position include Rosalynn Carter attending presidential cabinet meetings and testifying before a US Senate committee in support of mental health legislation, Nancy Reagan controlling her husband's schedule based on her consultations with an astrologer, and Hillary Clinton's leadership of a failed health care reform effort during her first year in the White House.

Michelle Obama and Melania Trump, just like all other first ladies, each endured a large amount of criticism. The press, the public, and particularly the opposition appeared to look for almost any excuse to publicly harangue the women performing what is arguably the most difficult unpaid job in American politics. Both Obama and Trump encountered backlash about their fashion choices, their purportedly expensive tastes, their political involvement (or lack thereof), and numerous other topics. One of the greatest difficulties that both women confronted was the highly partisan nature of the political environment during the eras in which they served. Many pundits took aim at Obama and Trump as a means of attacking their husbands and as a way to connect with left- or right-wing audience members. A second major challenge the two faced, and one unique to more modern first ladies, was the expanded media environment. The pervasiveness of social media meant that Obama and Trump encountered a new cacophony of critics because anyone with access to the internet became a potential commentator. In addition, the expectation that the women engage with the public through social media meant these contemporary first ladies were evaluated based upon new types of communicative behaviors.

In spite of the new media context in which both women operated as first lady, Michelle Obama and Melania Trump were assessed in ways that mimicked how past White House matrons were judged. They were accused of not behaving in a manner appropriate to the role by being unladylike or, more specifically, un-first-ladylike. They were also negatively gauged based on their perceived ability and desire to fulfill the obligations of the position. While most appraisals of the two were common critiques, Melania Trump did find herself occasionally embroiled in scandals, some of her own making and others instigated by her husband.

FAILING TO MEET THE STANDARDS FOR A FIRST LADY

Even though there are no clearly delineated standards of conduct for the spouse of a president, pretty much all of the women who have filled the role have at some point or other been accused of acting in a manner unbefitting the position. These types of claims are usually based on the long-held idea that the president's mate must serve as a role model for American women and embody the generally vague criteria for being a "good woman." Because what it means to be a good woman changes across time and from person to person, it is impossible for anyone to fully or continuously meet such a variable ideal. Still, complaints that a first lady is not behaving appropriately are some of the most prevalent criticisms of any president's wife.

Objections regarding the propriety of a presidential consort's en- actment of femininity often illustrate inconsistencies in the ways the women are appraised. Rosalynn Carter was faulted for being too thrifty and modest when she wore the same gown to Jimmy's presidential inau- gural ball that she had donned when he was elected governor of Georgia, yet just four years later the press reprimanded Nancy Reagan for being indulgent and ostentatious because her brand-new inaugural gown was too expensive. Laura Bush was simultaneously applauded and rebuked for choosing not to wear a headscarf in the Middle East—positive assess- ments called it a display of women's empowerment, and negative ones proclaimed it an insult to the host nation. She was later widely admon- ished for briefly putting on a headscarf she was given as a gift.

First ladies have also been rebuked for their decisions regarding the causes they champion. Despite the fact that first ladies tend to choose issues that fall well within the range of what are traditionally considered feminine concerns, their advocacy is still sometimes deemed problem- atic. Barbara Bush was commended for making literacy her signature cause, but when Laura Bush continued Barbara's work, critics argued that the former librarian lacked independence and creativity. They con- tended that she was merely mimicking the well-liked elder Bush rather than developing her own initiatives. In addition, after the September 11, 2001, terror attacks brought Laura Bush's attention to the plight of women in the Middle East, her decision to make international women's rights a major part of her advocacy agenda resulted in a great deal of censure. She was not berated for caring about the status and treatment of women, but she was scolded for seeming to overlook the inequities and injustices American women faced as she focused her attention on females abroad.

Michelle Obama and Melania Trump were each accused of not living up to the standards set for the first lady of the United States. Throughout her time in the White House, Obama constantly endured recrimination regarding her perceived ability to be a purportedly proper first lady. She dealt with objections to everything from her choice of shoes to her character to her personhood. Many of the concerns mirrored those stated about past first ladies, but others were clearly much more personal and often decidedly race-based. Over the first two years of her first ladyship, Trump also faced a great deal of criticism. She was similarly chided for her fashion choices, and denunciations of her personality were based on her apparent lack of a distinct, individual identity. Even though Trump was not subject to the same racially charged assessments as Obama, her personhood also came under fire on occasion when her physical attributes garnered negative attention. Although the types of criticisms the two women encountered were categorically identical, the applications of the indefinite criteria for the role resulted in distinct complaints about each woman. The critiques about Obama and Trump provide telling examples of the inconsistent ways in which these first ladies were judged.

It is not surprising that Michelle Obama and Melania Trump were frequently evaluated based on their appearance and were occasionally found wanting. Viewed as fashion icons, they each earned a large amount of positive attention due to the clothing they wore and the ways they carried themselves in public. However, along with the affirmations of their choices came disparaging assessments. Some writers rebuked Obama because of the diverse nature of her wardrobe. Compliments for her choices notwithstanding, many analysts found fault with the first lady because she failed to embrace a standardized dress code like many of her predecessors had. Pointing to Rosalynn Carter's A-line skirts and tucked-in blouses, Hillary Clinton's business suits, and Laura Bush's structured skirt suits, several pundits were bemused by Obama's mix of sundresses, slacks and cardigan sweater combos, and casual jeans and sneakers. Most journalists declared that the varied looks suited the first lady and aligned with her "everymom" persona, but a persistent group of primarily conservative reporters insisted that her attire was too distracting and that Obama was too vain to serve as a proper role model to young girls and women.

When Trump's public activity at the White House increased after her months-long stay in New York, the press immediately began assessing what many argued was her typical first lady uniform of a pencil skirt paired with a structured jacket or blouse and belt. Although she won praise from pundits who commented on the flattering lines and the seriousness of her appearance (a jab at Obama's ostensibly less businesslike mien), the press also censured Trump for her return to seemingly more predictable sartorial selections. Reporters deemed Trump's look uninventive, particularly for a former fashion model who had been touted as a cutting-edge "fashionista." She was castigated for not adequately fulfilling the expectations that, as first lady, she occupy the leading edge of women's fashion. These conflicting assessments of Obama and Trump indicate that when it comes to establishing a personal sense of style, the first lady can never win over all observers, no matter her approach.

In addition to evaluating how ladylike the president's wife looks, the press and public are habitually preoccupied with the cost of her wardrobe. Obama and Trump were each harangued for wearing expensive clothing—and also condemned for choosing more affordable garb. When it came to the pricey items, pundits either proclaimed that the outfits distanced the first ladies from the women they were expected to represent or that as role models the women set too high a benchmark for average Americans to meet. Melania Trump wearing a $51,000 Dolce & Gabbana jacket to the G-7 summit in Italy is one obvious example of high-priced clothing inciting criticism. Choosing an accessory worth more money than many Americans earn in a year gained the first lady contempt from both the US and international press. Similarly, Michelle Obama raised eyebrows in 2014 when she donned a gown valued at $12,000 for a state dinner at a time when the issue of income inequality had become a major talking point by her husband. The gown was event-appropriate, but the context drove critics to rebuff Obama's choice.

Complaints regarding the cost of the first lady's attire are routinely grounded in the ubiquitous misperception that clothing worn by the president's wife is bought with taxpayer funds. Objections of this nature are almost always based on either ignorance or partisanship, with more conservative commentators making inaccurate accusations about the wives of Democratic presidents and more liberal pundits leveling erroneous charges against the spouses of Republican commanders in chief.

The historical roots of stories about taxes being used to pay for the first lady's clothes can be traced at least as far back as Mary Todd Lincoln who did, in fact, use federal monies approved for the running and remodeling of the White House to purchase her expensive wardrobe. Past indiscretions notwithstanding, modern US first ladies do not receive any type of government subsidy to support their purchase of personal garments. Instead, they buy their own apparel or accept items as gifts. Jacqueline Kennedy's renowned wardrobe famously cost more per year to maintain than JFK earned as president. Kennedy enjoyed considerable financial support from her father-in-law, who did not want her appearance to be a political liability for John. Luckily, for women who cannot personally afford expensive gowns for events such as state dinners, designers frequently donate dresses and other outfits as gifts to the US government. Such items become part of the National Archives along with other presents government dignitaries receive.

Trump's seemingly expensive tastes were continually highlighted throughout her first couple of years in the White House; for example, the cost of her clothing was often compared to that of Obama's wardrobe. With multiple news articles highlighting the price difference between outfits each woman wore during similar events (e.g., Trump's $53,000 G-7 summit dress, coat, and shoes versus Obama's $474 G-20 summit skirt and sweater[1]), clear distinctions were made between the women. Based on the reported numbers, Trump spent between two and five times the amount Obama did on any given ensemble (the economic summit garment was an extreme outlier). As the wife of a purported billionaire, it makes sense that Trump might have worn pricier clothing, but that did not mitigate claims that her wealth and discernment made her less representative of and less relatable to American women than a first lady is expected to be.

Even though Obama and Trump were sometimes faulted for wearing lavish clothing, they were also occasionally pilloried for selecting more modestly priced items. Obama was known to wear off-the-rack pieces, and many commentators touted her decision to sport affordable garb as a nod to her upbringing and her connection to middle-class America. Still, her frugal choices were not always positively received. The press and the public slammed Obama for failing to meet the norms of propriety set for the first lady when she was photographed wearing shorts and sneakers while deplaning Air Force One for a family vacation. Despite the fact that she was heading on a hike in the Grand Canyon, politicos harangued Obama for appearing too casual, too comfortable, and too "common" for her position. A few years later, Obama listed the moment as her biggest fashion faux pas. Acknowledging the higher standards the president's wife is held to, she explained that she made the misstep because in that moment she was thinking like a mom heading on vacation with her family instead of like the first lady of the United States.[2]

Melania Trump earned herself a bit of praise for an affordable outfit she wore in the late summer of 2017. Donning a $300 casual pink ensemble from J. Crew on a return trip to the White House from Camp David, Trump was applauded for the elegant but simple look. Some critics maintained that she was copying Obama's casual attire, and others said she was awkwardly trying to appeal to a broad cross section of the American public, but most political analysts approved of her break from high-cost couture. A little over nine months later, she found herself embroiled in controversy when she selected a different inexpensive piece of clothing to travel in. The $39 "I REALLY DON'T CARE, DO U?" jacket she wore during a trip to tour detention centers for immigrant children separated from their families sparked widespread outrage (see chapter 3). The decision to wear the coat was considered puzzling by people who tried to decipher the meaning behind the words emblazoned on it. Several critics argued the message reflected Trump's attitude about her standing as the first lady, and many journalists and politicos wondered whether she was really suited for the job. The jacket inspired pundits to insist that the first lady was conducting herself in a manner unbecoming of her position in spite of the fact that she was taking action on a controversial subject.

In addition to the curiosity and criticism sparked by their clothing choices, Michelle Obama and Melania Trump were also routinely judged regarding aspects of their physical selves. These assessments were often not fair, reasonable, or kind. Obama endured objections based on her physical stature and her race, whereas Trump was censured for her seemingly indifferent countenance.

As the first African American first lady, Michelle Obama encountered a variety of criticisms that no other president's spouse before her did. Members of the mainstream press made remarks about her dark skin, height, and other attributes that allegedly prevented her from embodying the kind of femininity expected from a president's mate. Even though many discussions about her body were complimentary, including several articles highlighting how throngs of American women longed to have toned arms similar to Obama's, there were other conversations that depicted her physique as disturbingly unladylike. Reporters used words like "towering," "colossal," and "intimidating" to describe her almost-six-foot-tall frame. They pointed out that her sleeveless sheath dresses accentuated her arms and deemphasized her broad shoulders, that her decision to wear high-heeled shoes was unusual for a woman of her height, that her choice of color palette suited her dark skin tone, and that her sartorial style was an attempt to make her body seem more petite. Each such observation spotlighted the supposedly less feminine elements of her appearance.

Other outlandish complaints against Obama directly questioned her standing as a woman. Rumors that Michelle Obama had been born a man began during the 2008 campaign and persisted throughout her time in the White House. Later, conservative talk show hosts told viewers not only that Obama was not a woman but that she had committed murder in order to hide this fact from the public.[3] Although it might be easy to dismiss these pronouncements as absurd, thousands of people believed the diatribes, and the stories about Obama's sexuality became pervasive during her husband's second term in office. Some conservative editorial cartoonists began including subtle "bulges" or suggestive shadowing in her crotch area when drawing Michelle Obama, and several pundits began echoing these unfounded assertions when discussing the first lady. The allegations were so ubiquitous that, despite extensive articles by fact-checking websites debunking them, the assertions lingered for more than a decade.

In addition to having her womanhood challenged, Obama also encountered criticism that denied her basic humanity. On multiple occasions she was deemed unsuited to be first lady when she was equated with a primate. A West Virginia mayor called Obama an "ape in heels."[4] A schoolteacher in Georgia used social media to decry the first lady as a "poor gorilla" in need of a makeover.[5] A public official in the state of Washington claimed that "Gorilla Face Michelle" was only attractive to the "monkey man Barack."[6] Each person either resigned or was fired over his or her racist remarks, but the widespread nature of the sentiment indicated that a certain segment of the population viewed the first lady as subhuman. Although many past first ladies were harshly criticized (such as Hillary Clinton being called a "feminazi," an incarnation of Lady Macbeth, and a "man-hating fear-inspiring witch"), even the most derogatory portrayals generally depicted them as people. No other first lady had to withstand such vitriolic and dehumanizing attacks as Michelle Obama.

Melania Trump certainly was not as aggressively critiqued about her personhood as Michelle Obama was. However, during her first two years in the White House, she too was accused of not appropriately meeting the standards of the first ladyship based on her physical attributes, particularly her facial expressions. Starting during the presidential campaign but taking on new life the day her husband assumed the presidency, critical observations about Trump's countenance abounded.

Pictures of Trump at a breakfast event the morning of the inauguration showed her with different expressions that reporters identified as uninterested, distant, and upset. The assorted looks led to speculation regarding her assumed lack of interest in her new position and in her husband. Later that day, as images from the swearing-in ceremony emerged, reporters paid particular attention to Melania Trump's shifting demeanor during interactions with her husband. Her facial responsiveness earned her pity as well as condemnation. When it was thought that her husband had publicly scolded her, reporters and social media users alike conveyed concern for the new first lady and questioned the nature of the Trumps' marriage. Later, when Donald was delivering his national address, Melania was photographed with a vacant look on her face. At that point, commentators (particularly conservative ones) decried Trump's behavior and reproved her for not gazing supportively and lovingly at her husband as he outlined his vision for the country.

The various assessments of Melania Trump's facial expressions continued throughout her first couple of years in the White House. During her first trip to Europe, reporters said Trump looked depressed, seemed aloof, appeared bored, and gave the impression that she was deeply unhappy. As she prepared to host her first state dinner, Trump sported what many described as an insincere and overly practiced smile. When she was introduced to the president of Russia, Trump's so-called "look of terror" after shaking his hand provided material for a number of critical news stories and humorous late-night talk show monologues.

Several journalists tried to decode Trump's different looks and what some referred to as her "usual pose" (a downturned chin and very slightly opened mouth). They interpreted her expressions as strategically contrived attempts to hide her disdain for her situation or as habitual mannerisms ingrained when she was a model. These evaluations clearly implied that somehow her countenance was problematic and un-first-ladylike. Stories about her unenthusiastic expressions frequently included comparisons to her predecessors who had presented "permanent smiles" during public events.[7] Such references insinuated that Melania Trump's nonverbal displays violated the supportive and deferential ideals traditionally expected of a presidential helpmate. In reality, past White House matrons were generally much less fawning than the romanticized versions often recalled by those assessing the incumbent's spouse.

A large portion of the American population seemed to like Michelle Obama and appreciate her outgoing personality. Her willingness to be self-deprecating and her ability to adapt to various situations won her many fans. She earned favorability ratings as high as 72 percent and maintained an average positive score of 65 percent throughout her time in the White House.[8] She received lower ratings than both Barbara and Laura Bush but was better liked as first lady than Nancy Reagan or Hillary Clinton. In spite of her popularity, Obama was occasionally censured for her demeanor. Conservative pundits declared that she was too talkative and too often sought the spotlight at the expense of her husband. They said her frequent television appearances indicated that she was more interested in being a celebrity than in being an effective role model for America's female citizens. Such commentators argued that the first lady lacked the demure nature required of someone in the position and contrasted her against Laura Bush in order to highlight Obama's supposed dispositional shortcomings. Columnists quibbled about Michelle's tendency to joke about Barack, describing her gibes as inappropriate acts of aggression that violated the expectation for a president's wife to be resolutely supportive of her husband.

Some of the more biting judgments about Michelle Obama's character came from public figures holding extremely conservative viewpoints. Right-wing radio host Rush Limbaugh lambasted Obama as undisciplined, greedy, and power-hungry. He called her "Moochelle" to underscore his allegation that she selfishly indulged herself at the taxpayers' expense.[9] Many Republicans promulgated the idea that Obama was exceptionally pampered and ultimately unconcerned with average Americans' economic suffering by equating the first lady with Marie Antoinette. The contrived parallel accentuated Obama's supposed avarice and depicted her as out-of-touch with the electorate. Other GOP members chided Obama as hypocritical, contending that she did not adhere to the guidelines for being healthy that she supposedly tried to force others to follow.

The complaints regarding Melania Trump's disposition came largely from liberal analysts who ridiculed the first lady for not showing enough character. Pundits and politicos maintained that Trump was not adequately fulfilling the duties of the first lady because she was too much of a cipher and not enough of her own person. The extreme deference she generally showed her husband and her unwillingness to share her own opinions encouraged others to dismiss her as two-dimensional and flat. Liberal journalists objected that Trump was a negative role model for young women and girls because she appeared to value women's superficial features rather than their substantive skills and abilities. Some columnists even maintained that Trump's first ladyship could set the woman's movement back several decades. What most members of the press failed to note was that Trump did assert herself in important ways. For example, she refused to be pressured by custom or convention when she insisted on remaining in New York for the first few months of her husband's presidency. Journalists framed the move as an overindulged woman getting her way, but it was a show of strength by Trump because she refused to bend to tradition and instead prioritized the needs of her son.

Melania Trump's presumed lack of independence turned her rare displays of even the least bit of gumption into major news. On several occasions throughout her first two years in the White House, Trump refused to take her husband's offered hand. Each public instance caught on video spawned several mainstream news stories and spread quickly across social media sites. Her rejection of Donald was at times portrayed as Melania standing up to her purportedly overbearing husband. Critics, however, considered the rebuff an inappropriate act of petulance and admonished the first lady for creating a distraction and embarrassing her husband. This particular protest was lodged when Melania swatted away Donald's hand as they arrived in Saudi Arabia on their first presidential trip to the Middle East.

Michelle Obama and Melania Trump each endured numerous derogatory statements about their ladylikeness. Obama was deemed too tall, too black, and too aggressive, whereas Trump was too passive, too superficial, and too aloof. The fundamental unfairness of many of the claims regarding the feminine attributes enacted by Obama and Trump is apparent in the inconsistencies of the appraisals. Obama was reprimanded for baring her arms, but when Trump went sleeveless, no one complained. Trump was lambasted for being too quiescent, whereas Obama's activity earned her reproach. Obama's wardrobe was said to contain too many off-the-rack pieces, and Trump's was deemed to have too few.

OVERSTEPPING AND UNDERPERFORMING

One particularly unfair type of charge leveled against a first lady has to do with how well she executes the duties of the position. Grievances about her job performance are usually grounded in how willingly and competently she participates in the various assumed, but not explicitly stated, responsibilities of the president's spouse, such as serving as the national hostess, championing appropriate causes, and being the compassionate face of the government. There are no formal guidelines for the job itself, but that does not prevent the press and public from judging the women who occupy the East Wing based on unstated and equivocal measures of effectiveness.

Objections about how first ladies approach the role tend to take two opposing perspectives. The women are either charged with overstepping the invisible boundaries of their position, or they are faulted for underperforming in their capacity as the national matriarch. Very few women of the past have managed to find an acceptable balance between the demand to be an enthusiastic public servant and the need to appear unassertive. Women who have failed to achieve the right blend of activity and deference have been rebuked for their behaviors. Rosalynn Carter, Nancy Reagan, and Hillary Clinton were all berated for being too ambitious; Carter and Clinton were said to be too involved in policy development, whereas Reagan was accused of meddling in the running of her husband's administration. On the other end of the spectrum are the women who have been reprimanded for not adequately fulfilling expectations for someone in the role. Far fewer women tend to be denounced for not being aggressive enough than for being overly so, yet because modern first ladies are expected to be more active than their earlier counterparts, presidential consorts must guard against charges of inactivity. Not since Mamie Eisenhower has a first lady been able to refrain from engaging in some sort of public social advocacy without facing harsh criticism.

Michelle Obama and Melania Trump took different approaches to fulfilling their responsibilities as first lady. Obama was decidedly more active and outgoing from the start, and Trump was more sedate and reserved. Within the first few months of their time in the White House, Obama was admonished by pundits and politicos for reaching beyond the limits of the position, and Trump was lambasted for not doing enough. In truth, the inability of either woman to adequately navigate the unstated expectations of the position is not surprising because unclear responsibilities are difficult for anyone to effectively discharge. Equally unsurprising is the fact that a deep partisan divide undergirded many of the criticisms of Obama and Trump.

There were a series of grievances related to Obama's job performance as the first lady. Some revolved around her alleged prodigality. For example, her lavish first state dinner was said by critics to indicate her purported willingness to overspend federal funds. Other complaints focused on what some commentators referred to as her apparent preoccupation with fame. These types of reproach accused Obama of using the White House to cultivate friendships with prominent actors and musicians in hopes of solidifying her own status as a celebrity. Such protests were relatively minor in scope and had little impact on her overall public persona. However, the admonishment she suffered regarding her assertive social advocacy was much more sustained and created problems for the first lady.

As explained in chapter 3, Michelle Obama's primary initiative was the *Let's Move!* campaign that intended to help encourage kids to lead healthier lives. The effort to promote better eating and exercise habits was relatively well received by the public at large. It was a kid-friendly endeavor that fit squarely within the parameters of Obama's established "everymom" persona. Once the program moved beyond encouragement and role modeling to include supporting legislation, however, Obama encountered significant pushback. Critics claimed she was exceeding the boundaries of her position by interfering with governmental decisions. Even though she did not testify before any congressional committees as Rosalynn Carter had done or head a commission like Hillary Clinton did, conservative pundits said Michelle Obama's public support for a rider to a bill funding school lunches was an overreach for the first lady. The objection assumed that she should refrain from remarking on government actions because she was married to the president. Obama's use of her rhetorical power was apparently offensive to those who believed the president's mate should serve as a model of female deference.

The *Let's Move!* campaign was not the only bit of advocacy for which Michelle Obama received criticism. Her use of the first lady pulpit was also a point of contention when she helped develop *Let Girls Learn*, an initiative designed to increase girls' access to education around the world. Some conservative columnists labeled the program sexist because it did not include males, and others protested that its global focus was troublesome because it diverted attention and energy away from American needs. Essentially, critiques about Obama's *Let Girls Learn* framed the president's wife as setting the wrong priorities and attending to problems that were outside her purview. This grousing about Obama and her project was clearly a result of partisan gameplay because many of the same people rebuking Obama for *Let Girls Learn* had previously applauded Laura Bush for her work drawing attention to the plight of women in the Middle East. The selective use of the "overstepping" charge is another clear indication that the first lady of the United States is not a clearly defined position, nor is it as apolitical as some people might believe.

During the first two years she was in the White House, Melania Trump was certainly not accused of reaching beyond the limits of her position as first lady. In fact, most criticisms of Trump fell on the other end of the spectrum; she was often faulted for inadequately performing the duties of the president's wife. Quibbling about Trump's purported ineffectiveness as first lady began before her husband took the oath of office. When she announced that her move to Washington, DC, would be delayed, she immediately opened herself up to objections about her ability to serve as an effective presidential consort. When she trimmed the Office of the First Lady staff to what some called a skeleton crew, critics again argued that she was not planning to fulfill the duties of the job. Although Trump did host several White House events, held meetings with her staff, engaged in charitable works, visited schools and hospitals (i.e., did the things widely expected of any first lady) while she was technically residing in New York, she was still accused of not doing enough. After she moved into the White House full-time, the perceptions of her inadequate activity persisted. Part of the reason was the delayed announcement of her advocacy campaign.

Unlike many first ladies who establish their signature initiatives or causes before or shortly after entering the White House, Melania Trump waited more than a year to unveil her program; it was not until May of 2018 that she presented *Be Best* to the nation (see chapter 3). The announcement had been expected months earlier, and two scheduled press conferences regarding the initiative had been postponed. Critics, particularly liberal commentators, maintained the delay was an indication of Trump's lack of interest in both her position as first lady and in helping others. Such charges were reinforced when *Be Best* was revealed as a campaign to draw attention to already existing efforts by others rather than as a novel initiative in its own right. Trump was said to lack the creativity and entrepreneurialism expected of a modern first lady. Ironically, being creative and entrepreneurial were characteristics that drew criticism for several of her predecessors, including Michelle Obama.

Melania Trump's performance as the first lady became an issue again when she seemed to vanish for several weeks in the spring of 2018. In May, she underwent what was described as a minor medical procedure for a kidney problem. After her brief hospitalization, Trump made no public appearances, nor did she do any public outreach, for about three weeks. There were no photos of her, no social media posts from her, and no public interactions of any discernable sort by her during that time. People on mainstream and social media began counting the days since she had last been seen. Jokesters hung missing-person posters bearing Trump's photo and description around New York and DC. Columnists underscored the unusual nature of such inactivity on an almost daily basis. The episode reignited concerns about Trump's dedication to serving as the White House matriarch. In addition, reporters wondered if she was hiding in order to avoid fallout from the bungled *Be Best* launch. The so-called disappearance also brought back questions regarding the Trump marriage because Melania's apparent sequestering happened just as new information was released regarding an alleged affair her husband had with a porn star shortly after Melania had given birth to the couple's son.

Rumors swirled about Melania Trump's absence that ranged from speculation she'd had plastic surgery to assertions she was working on divorce papers to tales about Donald having killed her in order to avoid paying a divorce settlement. Aside from the careless gossip, more considered and critical assessments of the situation declared the absence, no matter the cause, unacceptable. Pundits argued that Trump's failure to make herself available even for a simple photograph or two created a social and political distraction that could be construed as a dereliction of her duties as the first lady. This perspective underscored the idea that somehow, although the person is unelected and unpaid, the first lady is not entitled to any privacy once she moves into the nation's most famous residence.

Like Melania Trump, Michelle Obama also endured complaints that she underperformed as the first lady of the United States. Such claims came from two very different groups. First, there were the conservative politicos who revived critiques that had emerged during the 2008 campaign that Obama was not patriotic enough to be an effective first lady. They contended that, as the president's wife, Michelle Obama failed to show enough gratitude and concern for her nation. These grievances took many forms. In 2011, GOP operatives began circulating eventually debunked stories of Obama grumbling about having to attend a 9/11 memorial event. The first lady was said to have whispered, "All this for a damned flag" while at the commemoration. Despite the fact that these allegations were soundly refuted, right-wing pundits routinely repeated the accusations as part of a sustained effort to paint Obama as an ineffective first lady. When Obama launched her *Let Girls Learn* campaign as a global effort, critics used the international focus as an indicator that Obama did not care enough about her own country. Some reactionary commentators accused her of not engaging in adequate and appropriate action as the first lady because she was more concerned about poor girls in Africa than homeless American military veterans. These recriminations overlooked Obama's extensive work supporting US military members and their families, underscoring their deep partisan roots.

The second group that charged Obama with being less than effective as first lady was a bit more unexpected. Some liberal feminists argued that Obama did not fulfill the responsibilities of her position because she did not provide adequate role modeling for American women, particularly young girls, due to her adoption of the "mom-in-chief" persona. They objected to her decision to downplay her academic and professional successes in favor of accentuating her work as a mother and supportive spouse. Conceding that the move might have been necessary in order to quell some of the race-based challenges Obama faced, these critics still proclaimed the move unacceptable because the first lady was not showing young girls that they could aspire to be something other than wives and mothers. To be clear, they were not opposed to pointing out the value of being a wife or mother, but they were troubled by the fact that those elements of Obama's life were highlighted at the expense of providing a more encompassing picture of her multifaceted and accomplished background. They protested that Obama was presenting a rather narrow view of womanhood and a stunted perspective on femininity. These same observers made similar assertions about Trump, maintaining that she was not simply neglecting her duties in this regard, but that she was actively disempowering future generations of women by teaching them that female submissiveness results in wealth and fame.

As high-profile women, both Michelle Obama and Melania Trump endured complaints about the management of ambiguous duties as first lady. All of their decisions were bound to be problematic to some segment of the diverse population evaluating their every move. Critiques about them made it clear that if a president's wife tries to retain some privacy and stay out of the public eye, she is harangued. However, if she tries to use her attention-getting position to help others, she opens herself up to charges of not doing enough, helping the wrong people, or being too ambitious. When it comes to fulfilling the functions of such an undefined role, no woman is safe from accusations of either overstepping or underperforming as the first lady of the United States.

MANAGING SCANDALS

First ladies often find themselves in the midst of a scenario where criticisms lead to more substantial, more sustained, and more widespread disparagements of their behaviors or the conduct of those around them. In these cases, the wives of presidents might labor to negotiate a full-fledged scandal. Many past White House matrons have created their own difficult situations. The financial improprieties Mary Todd Lincoln committed typify the self-created ordeal. Others include Florence Harding meddling in her husband's appointee process and Nancy Reagan refusing to return borrowed clothes, failing to properly register sartorial gifts, and ignoring other protocols regarding her expensive wardrobe.

In addition to being called out for their own bad acts, some first ladies have suffered through public accusations of misdeeds by the president. Jacqueline Kennedy and Hillary Clinton endured rumors of sexual misconduct by their husbands. Nancy Reagan dealt with fallout over her husband's Iran Contra affair and assertions regarding Ronald's dementia during his last years in the White House. Perhaps one of the most well-known modern scandals was Watergate. Pat Nixon had largely been kept in the dark by her husband and learned about the problem by reading the newspaper. In the end, she had to withstand the disgrace of leaving the White House after her husband was forced to resign because of his wrongdoing.

Even though there were plenty of criticisms leveled at Michelle Obama during her eight years presiding over the East Wing, she was never directly accused of any impropriety that rose to the level of a scandal. Compared to the four administrations before Barack Obama took office, there were relatively few major controversies in the Obama White House, and none that reflected poorly on Michelle Obama. She never had to defend her husband against allegations of sexual or financial misconduct, was not charged with violating the law, and did not break with the accepted social mores of the era. Other members of the Obama White House were questioned about their role in troubling events like the attack on the US embassy in Benghazi and purportedly problematic decision-making by IRS officials, but aside from some debunked race- and partisan-based efforts to discredit Michelle Obama, the first lady was never entangled in a scandal of her own making. She only became tangentially involved with one of someone else's creation when Melania Trump delivered a speech to the Republican National Convention (RNC) in the summer of 2016 that contained parts of a 2008 address by Obama (see chapter 1). Melania Trump, on the other hand, found herself managing accusations of inappropriate behavior from the start of the 2016 campaign and throughout her time in the East Wing.

Melania Trump confronted a variety of improper actions during her first several months as first lady, some by her but most by her husband. As delineated in chapter 1, during the campaign, she was directly accused of misconduct when nude photos of her circulated around the internet and stories about her work as an illegal immigrant in the United States emerged. Later, she was charged with lacking an effective moral compass when she delivered an RNC speech she said she had written herself that contained passages that matched Michelle Obama's 2008 Democratic National Convention (DNC) address. Trump's speech raised serious concerns because the episode included initial lies about authorship, clear instances of plagiarism, and an attempted cover-up complete with efforts to shift blame and avoid taking responsibility for the bad behavior.

In addition to her own wrongdoing, throughout the 2016 campaign Trump also endured accusations of immoral behavior by her husband. Although there were several charges of misdeeds by Donald, Melania Trump was most directly connected to two sex-related scandals because the usually reticent woman chose to defend her husband. In one case, when an *Access Hollywood* tape of Donald was released in which he used vulgar language about women and bragged about engaging in sexually harassing activities, Melania dismissed his banter as "locker room talk" in a series of interviews. Her denial that his attitudes were troubling embroiled Trump in controversy as critics argued she was condoning the mistreatment of women. These assertions were amplified when her husband was later directly accused of sexually assaulting several women. When those allegations broke, Melania Trump dismissed the purported victims as liars. Trump's defense of her husband became an issue because it contravened her professed desire to be an advocate for women. In addition, her support for her husband was similar to the defense Hillary Clinton mounted on behalf of Bill Clinton in the 1990s, a stance that Donald Trump used to frame Hillary Clinton as a fraudulent feminist who harmed women. Melania Trump's actions in light of the condemnation of Clinton opened the campaign and the future first lady to further accusations of hypocrisy.

The scandals Melania Trump weathered during the presidential campaign were a precursor to the multiple controversies she had to negotiate throughout her time in the White House. Within the first two years of her husband's presidency, Trump again was condemned for plagiarism and again found herself defending her husband against accusations of sexual misconduct. In addition, some key political actions by her husband and members of his administration created additional problems for the first lady.

The second time members of the press maintained that Melania Trump stole significant portions of work from Michelle Obama occurred when she unveiled her *Be Best* initiative (see chapter 3). One of the documents released as part of her effort to help parents teach kids to navigate social media was identical to one disseminated by the Obama administration. Michelle Obama had not created the document, as many journalists and commentators erroneously declared, and Melania Trump never professed to have written it or to have commissioned its writing, but the public was quick to berate Trump for once more stealing from Obama. This contrived conflict was problematic for Trump because her earlier behaviors made the charge of plagiarism eminently believable to her critics, even though in this case the charge was unwarranted.

The sex scandals that plagued Donald Trump during the latter part of his presidential campaign continued and expanded during his presidency. As he was fighting lawsuits brought by his putative sexual assault victims, new information came to light regarding a payoff one of his attorneys made to a porn star in order to hide a consensual sexual affair Donald had with her. It was revealed that, one month prior to the election, Trump's lawyer gave the woman known as Stormy Daniels $130,000 to sign a nondisclosure agreement so she would not share details of the tryst she'd had with Donald Trump. Although the fling had happened years earlier, the payment was intended to avoid adding fuel to the media firestorm surrounding Trump's *Access Hollywood* tape and sexual assault accusations. When the story about the Daniels-Trump affair and cover-up finally did break, it was a prominent part of the news for the first several weeks of Donald Trump's administration. A full year after the revelations about the payment surfaced, the affair remained in the national spotlight.

Melania Trump was drawn into the scandal when it was revealed that the liaison took place shortly after the first lady had given birth to her and Donald's son, Barron. Reporters clamored for a response from Mrs. Trump but none was forthcoming. Unlike her proactive defense of Donald's vulgar taped conversation, Melania was largely silent about the Daniels affair. The first statement by the Office of the First Lady regarding the scandal was released more than a year into the ongoing coverage. The comment was not about Melania Trump's feelings or thoughts and contained no defense of or possible explanation for the affair or payoff. Instead, it was a simple post on Twitter from the first lady's spokeswoman asking reporters to leave the couple's minor son out of the news. After that brief remark, nothing more was heard from the first lady or her staff regarding the ongoing drama for several weeks.

Trump was once more dragged into the situation in June 2018 when another of Donald Trump's lawyers, former New York mayor Rudy Giuliani, insisted that the first lady accepted her husband's version of events and was supportive of the president. Instead of quietly letting the statement pass, Melania Trump's spokeswoman contested the claim. The first lady's representative did not make any statements about Trump's perspectives but simply retorted that Trump had not revealed her feelings to Giuliani. Though the comment did not clarify Trump's position regarding her husband's infidelity, many members of the media assumed the denial of Giuliani's assertions, coupled with Trump's refusal to explicitly support her husband, implied that the first lady did not condone Donald's behavior.

In May 2018, the Trump administration reinterpreted a federal law regarding illegal immigrants to justify the separation of children from their parents when caught entering the United States without proper documentation. Within a few weeks, over two thousand minor children had been placed in makeshift detention centers in Arizona and Texas. The kids had no contact with their parents, and there were many accusations that their rights had been violated in a variety of ways and that their safety had been compromised in the facilities. By the middle of June, the situation had raised such concern that numerous social and governmental leaders spoke out against the practice of family separations and the United Nations condemned the policy as inhumane. The past first ladies, each of whom had championed social platforms that centered on children and families, became vocal critics denouncing the US government's actions. Rosalynn Carter called it "disgraceful and a shame to our country."[10] Laura Bush wrote an op-ed in which she compared the separations to the US internment of Japanese-Americans during World War II—what she called "one of the most shameful episodes in U.S. history."[11] Hillary Clinton dubbed the situation a "humanitarian crisis," and Michelle Obama publicly supported Bush's statement, adding, "Sometimes truth transcends party."[12]

The widespread negative coverage of the Trump administration's actions drew a great deal of attention, and Melania Trump was quickly called out for not having made any public remarks and presumably no private efforts to intervene. As the past first ladies spoke up, journalists pointed out the lack of a statement from the sitting first lady, who was both a self-professed advocate for children and a former illegal immigrant herself. Within twenty-four hours of the consistent and forceful messaging from her predecessors, Trump's spokeswoman declared, "Mrs. Trump hates to see children separated from their families."[13] The comment was hailed by some as Melania Trump taking a brave stance against her husband and mocked by others as a hollow, impotent utterance that took no clear position on the specific actions by the president. Two days later, as protests continued to expand and President Trump decided to ostensibly soften the policy's implementation, journalists and pundits credited the first lady with privately pressing the issue and encouraging Donald's change of heart.

The separations did not actually stop after her alleged intervention, nor were children effectively reunited with their families in large numbers for weeks afterward, but the press still maintained that Melania Trump helped resolve the situation and mitigate the scandal. Building on the positive press, Trump decided to visit a shelter in Texas where some of the children were being housed. Unfortunately, her choice of attire dominated coverage of the visit after she donned the now-infamous green "I REALLY DON'T CARE, DO U?" coat for the trip. The piece of clothing called into question her sincerity and raised concerns that her apparent efforts on behalf of the children were nothing more than a publicity ploy. When many children had still not been reunited with their families weeks later, some liberal analysts suggested the message on the jacket had been more revealing than anyone at the time wanted to believe.

Melania Trump had to navigate several small-to-moderate and a few large-scale scandals during her time as a presidential candidate's wife, as the spouse of the president-elect, and as the first lady of the United States. Her general method for managing such matters was to remain silent, but when that was not an option, she usually sent her staff members to speak on her behalf. It is not possible to gauge whether her use of a spokesperson was intended to avoid problems based on her fluent but not flawless English, or if it was perhaps a means of retaining some personal plausible deniability. Whatever the motive, Trump's distanced and reticent approach did decrease the chances for the muck of scandal to directly soil the position of first lady.

All women who serve as the first lady of the United States must contend with disapproval of one sort or another. Because there is no formal job description for the position, evaluations of a first lady's performance take myriad forms, and criteria for assessing her effectiveness shift often. Thus, critiques are unavoidable, and all a president's spouse can really control is her own response to the various compliments and insults she experiences. Michelle Obama and Melania Trump both received a lot of objections about numerous aspects of their first ladyships. From clothing to personality, from skin color to facial expressions, from undue assertiveness to frustrating silence and submissiveness, virtually every facet of these women's beings garnered negative attention from mainstream or social media at some point.

Michelle Obama and Melania Trump approached the criticisms against them in a way many past first ladies had in that they generally ignored the chatter. This strategy worked for Trump, who had cultivated a persona that left no one surprised by her silence. Even when serious subjects like family separations at the border forced the first lady to make a statement, Trump usually sent brief remarks through her spokesperson instead of addressing the press or the public directly. Michelle Obama also regularly ignored disparaging statements about her. Yet, because she often made herself accessible to the media, Obama was frequently questioned about the grievances lodged against her. When directly confronted, she sometimes sidestepped the query by changing the subject, dismissing the comments as people having different opinions, or laughing off the affront with some self-deprecating gibe. On rare occasions, Obama did grapple with criticisms head on and used them as teachable moments in order to help kids learn about bullying, to open a dialogue about race relations in the United States, or to demonstrate the struggles women face in their fight for equality. However, these responses usually occurred within very specific contexts and were not the norm. By routinely ignoring the majority of the attempts to discredit them, both Michelle Obama and Melania Trump defused the attacks and prevented most from gaining more traction and attention.

The opprobrium that the two most recent first ladies endured is interesting for a number of reasons beyond the simple stir of gossip. The varied and inconsistent nature of the complaints about Michelle Obama and Melania Trump are good indicators of the continued uncertainty Americans have regarding women's role in society and politics. Like many of the presidents' spouses before them, these women were asked to do the impracticable by representing an ideal of American womanhood that meets the presumptions of all citizens. It is impossible for any first lady to embody the quintessential American woman because there is no consensus as to what that should be.

Whenever a first lady demonstrates the complex nature of modern womanhood by being something other than a supportive wife and doting mother (or grandmother), she encounters protests from those who prefer a narrow interpretation of femininity. In addition, if she fully embraces the conventional roles of wife and mother, she opens herself to censure for not representing independent, empowered women. What's more, because customary and outdated assumptions about women's roles habitually undergird the assessments of presidential spouses, women like Obama and Trump are continually evaluated based on a limited understanding of the position. It is difficult for any real woman to escape criticism when she is expected to embody a caricature of multiple, dated versions of American femininity.

The faultfinding directed against Michelle Obama and Melania Trump reveals just how politicized the purportedly apolitical position of the first lady of the United States really is. Customarily, the party holding the White House asserts that the first ladyship is or should be a position free from the partisan jockeying of Washington, DC, because it is not a position spouses seek through their own election but one they are forced into by virtue of their marriage to the president. Still, it is clear that members of both dominant political parties drag presidential consorts into the political fray, whether they are willing or not. The haranguing Michelle Obama and Melania Trump each endured illustrates just how much first ladies are used in the political gamesmanship of the modern era. Because presidential helpmates are now essentially pushed into public service through social advocacy, they are always tied to an issue or cause that can become divisive. Obama's seemingly party-neutral effort to encourage children to lead healthier lives somehow became objectionable. Trump's attempt to simply draw attention to the good works of other organizations likewise resulted in recrimination.

As Obama's eight and Trump's first two years as first lady indicate, a contemporary presidential spouse cannot avoid censure by remaining out of the public eye—in fact, she might earn more disapproval for her absence—and she can be attacked for any activity she takes part in. The public and political nature of being the president's mate makes it impossible to please all of the people any of the time. To negotiate life in the White House, the first lady must grow the proverbial thick skin and learn to live with criticism as she forges her own path and makes her own decisions about her level of engagement. As the next chapter explains, maneuvering through public life as first lady includes negotiating how active to be during the president's almost inevitable pursuit of a second term in office.

FIVE

Presidential Election, Round Two

Campaigning as First Lady

THE PRESIDENT'S WIFE HAS ALWAYS RECEIVED A GREAT DEAL OF attention from the press and the public. Despite the difficulties contemporary first ladies have faced managing expectations, most have earned higher favorability ratings than their husbands. Thus, when it comes time for an incumbent president to seek a second term in office, the first lady is often considered a valuable asset for the campaign. During a reelection bid, the White House matron is routinely tasked with winning over women voters and humanizing the president. The first lady is a particularly useful campaign operative because she is believed to have intimate knowledge of what it takes to be president and because she commands more media attention than a challenger's wife. Modern presidential spouses have generally been active campaigners, but the history of sitting first ladies buoying their husbands' reelection efforts extends beyond the current era.

Even before social conventions allowed women to advocate for their husbands, assertive first ladies and inventive campaign staffers found ways to insert presidential consorts into an incumbent's pursuit of a second term in office. Some of the activities the women engaged in were subtle and fell within the realm of acceptable endeavors for first ladies. Louisa Adams, wife of John Quincy Adams, arranged many dinners and receptions in support of her husband's ultimately unsuccessful effort to retain the White House. Julia Grant helped her husband's reelection effort by interacting with newsmen and sharing stories about the Grant family's life that she believed revealed Ulysses's most positive qualities and helped the American public relate to the "White House family." In addition, many first ladies accompanied their husbands on tours of various parts of the United States that also functioned as campaign trips.

The twentieth century witnessed an increase in women's political empowerment and in the ways sitting first ladies participated in presidential campaigns. In 1912, Helen Taft attended the Republican National Convention (RNC) to celebrate her husband's nomination, but she also visited the Democratic National Convention (DNC) to prevent the opposition from harshly criticizing her spouse. Her presence at the DNC did suppress the grievances articulated against William Taft at that gathering, but William still lost control of the Oval Office. Twenty-eight years later, Eleanor Roosevelt became the first incumbent's mate to address delegates at a presidential nominating convention when she delivered a speech to the DNC in Chicago. Although she did not mention her husband by name or by title, many people credit Franklin D. Roosevelt's third Democratic nomination to the first lady's oration.

The second half of the twentieth century brought an expansion of campaign activity by sitting first ladies. In 1964, Claudia "Lady Bird" Johnson embarked on an eight-state tour of the southern United States during which she encouraged people to support the Civil Rights Act and to vote for her husband. Her popularity and southern roots made her an effective ambassador for the president. She traveled without her husband and received a generally warm welcome at each stop. Her successor, Pat Nixon, followed suit and did a great deal of solo campaigning on behalf of her husband Richard's reelection in 1972. Betty Ford's popularity led to a grassroots movement in which partisans argued not in favor of Gerald Ford but in support of "Betty's husband for president." Betty Ford was such an integral part of Gerald's campaign that, when he lost to Jimmy Carter, Betty delivered his concession speech; the president was said to have lost his voice in the final hours of campaigning. In 1992, Barbara Bush became the first Republican first lady to deliver a full convention address to the RNC. (Pat Nixon and Nancy Reagan each made brief comments in 1972 and 1984, respectively, but neither presented a prepared oration.) Bush also served as a behind-the-scenes adviser and as a surrogate who campaigned with and without her husband.

All first ladies from Barbara Bush to Michelle Obama have actively participated in their husbands' reelection campaigns by giving speeches, attending fund-raisers, sitting for interviews, appearing in advertisements, and being highly visible (and usually very vocal) during conventions. It remains to be seen what kind of first lady campaigner Melania Trump will be, but the advantages and disadvantages of being a president's wife during the contest offer insights into potential strategies Trump might use in 2020. Obama's actions as a presidential helpmate during the 2012 campaign, as well as the behaviors of some of the other women who have overseen the East Wing during a reelection race, demonstrate various approaches to balancing the needs of being the first lady with the demands of acting as a campaign surrogate. These examples offer touchstones for Melania Trump as she contemplates her potential role in the 2020 election.

THE ADVANTAGES OF INCUMBENCY

All sitting first ladies enjoy a variety of inherent benefits when it comes to participating in their husbands' reelection campaigns. These perks include having a successful campaign to learn from, easy access to the media, and an established personal staff. Not all East Wing matrons draw on the advantages of being an incumbent in the same way, but presidential spouses do have more resources at their disposal when situated in the White House than they did when they were a challenger's mate.

One of the most valuable assets a first lady can draw on for a reelection campaign is her experience. With the exception of the women who assumed the position as their husbands ascended to the Oval Office to complete someone else's term (e.g., Betty Ford became first lady when Gerald Ford replaced Richard Nixon), most presidents' wives have already endured the informal vetting process the media puts all candidates' wives through. The women who have previously survived a successful campaign have been complimented and critiqued by a wide range of people, have committed their share of gaffes and missteps, and have developed their own public image. By maneuvering through the initial campaign and negotiating life in the White House, most of the women learned through trial and error how to exercise the rhetorical power that becomes their most effective tool for managing the ambiguous job of first lady. Of course, the women engaged with the public in different ways during their first campaign, so each had a distinct well of experience to draw from. For example, Barbara Bush's largely positive media treatment in 1988 made for more relaxed and amiable interactions in 1992, but Hillary Clinton's rather contentious portrayals in 1992 left her struggling to reform her image throughout the 1996 race.

During a reelection campaign, first ladies are usually much more savvy about wielding the power of the first lady pulpit than they were during their husbands' initial presidential run. This means they are more cautious about the words they choose, more mindful about their relationships with members of the media, and more aware of how their established personas influence the ways members of the press and public interpret their actions. Experience helps first ladies be better campaigners, but it does not make them flawless political operatives. Laura Bush was a much more vocal participant in George W. Bush's reelection campaign than she was during his initial presidential run. While many journalists described her increased activity as a sign of her political awakening and empowerment, several others argued that her activity was a mercenary attempt by the campaign to take improper advantage of her good nature and popularity. Her performances were just as frequently chided for appearing overly scripted and insincere as they were applauded as displays of independence.

In 2012, Michelle Obama capitalized on her experiences both as a seasoned national campaigner and as a sitting first lady. She managed to sidestep some of the problems she'd confronted as a challenger's wife in 2008. More aware of the impact of sound bites and the ways comments can be taken out of context, Obama avoided making statements that the opposition could use to frame her as unpatriotic, angry, or aggressive. Some journalists mentioned her 2008 remarks about finally being proud of her country (see chapter 1) as an example of her previous public errors, and many opponents tried to dredge up past critiques in an effort to discredit her, but there were no new controversies regarding poorly phrased or misunderstood expressions from Obama during the 2012 campaign. Instead, the first lady was described as gracious, eloquent, amiable, and an effective advocate for her husband.

Michelle Obama also turned positive lessons from 2008 into effective strategies for her own image management in 2012. Playing up her embrace of traditional gender roles, Obama took advantage of her well-known "everymom" persona and pushed the concept to fresh heights by presenting herself as the nation's "mom-in-chief." She had diverted attention away from her standing as a successful professional woman and toward her actions as a doting mother and supportive wife early in the 2008 campaign, and she continued to make her domesticity a core tenet of her public profile throughout her time as first lady. Therefore, when she hit the campaign trail in 2012, it made sense to double down on the established image. She underscored her maternal interests by greeting children at various events, routinely speaking about her daughters, and using her motherly point of view as grounds for discussing political topics. During the campaign, Obama often used the phrase "as a mother" to build her credibility and to associate herself with a wide cross section of female voters. By repeatedly talking about the challenges of raising children in the White House, Obama reaffirmed that she prioritized motherhood and subtly reminded listeners about her unique insights into the presidency.

Melania Trump was not a very active campaigner during the 2016 campaign, but that does not mean there weren't lessons for her to learn from the experience. Her negative insertion into the contest was a clear indication that no matter how quiet she remained, she could not escape being drawn into the campaign. As the 2020 race evolves, she should understand that she cannot remove herself from the fanfare simply by not participating. The critiques of her from her husband's first run will undoubtedly reemerge during his reelection bid as reporters remind voters about Trump's nude photos, the questions about her immigration status when she began working in the United States, and her purported acts of plagiarism. Trump's strategy of ignoring concerns about her past worked out okay for her husband in 2016, but it harmed her public image and contributed to her unusually negative favorability ratings.

If Trump is at all concerned about her own legacy, she must more effectively balance her needs as a public figure and as a private citizen. The desire for privacy might push her to be more reserved in public, but being too unforthcoming creates problems. As she should have learned from the 2016 campaign, a lack of communicativeness leads to journalists and pundits making negative assumptions about her and leaves the public little upon which to build bonds with her. The reticent persona she developed in 2016 encouraged people to interpret her through the lens of her husband rather than as her own individual person. Instead of speaking only to defend her husband as she did in 2016, in her second effort as a candidate's spouse, Trump should also engage in a little proactive and reactive self-defense. Telling the public a bit more about her past could help contextualize the photos and her immigration status while simultaneously offering points of connection between herself and the audience. Strategically discussing her background could create a more concrete image of Trump as a multifaceted woman and encourage empathetic feelings from voters. In addition, rather than hiding from accusations of misconduct, she should face the more public and potentially enduring ones directly. Although it is too late now, she should have apologized for plagiarizing from Michelle Obama's 2008 speech. The public is more likely to forgive and forget such an act if the aftermath of the offense is managed effectively. Ignoring a situation or trying to cover it up leads to more coverage and longer-lasting problems. If Trump finds herself in another situation where her morality and intelligence are widely debated, she should learn from the past and acknowledge the concerns, explain the situation, and apologize (if appropriate) rather than avoiding the issue.

Sitting first ladies learn more from their first presidential campaigns and time in the East Wing than just how to avoid controversy and leverage their public personas. Being able to wield their rhetorical power requires that they also learn how to finesse their relationship with the press. Presidential spouses have used various strategies for managing the media. Some have recognized reporters as allies in their efforts to draw attention to causes and issues, and others have treated journalists as prying entities that regrettably must be endured. Most first ladies have tried to strike a balance between giving enough access that reporters treat them fairly and still retaining some degree of privacy for themselves and their families. The connections presidents' mates build with members of the media are always important, but they become particularly impactful during a reelection campaign because these associations inform how the first lady's actions get covered. Presidential consorts are able to earn significant free media coverage for their husbands' campaigns by virtue of their position, but the attention they receive could just as easily be negative as positive.

Michelle Obama had a largely constructive relationship with the mainstream media that spanned a variety of outlets and formats. She invited members of the traditional press to events at the White House and gave interviews at reasonable intervals. She also made numerous appearances on television programs considered "soft" news shows, such as *Good Morning America* and *Today*. She went on daytime and late-night talk and variety shows, made guest cameos on scripted television, and promoted her health and wellness initiatives on fitness-focused reality television programs like *The Biggest Loser*. Obama sat for interviews with feature writers from major magazines, contributed to parenting blogs, and posted videos on the internet. She also managed a social media micro-blogging account on Twitter where she occasionally answered questions from the public. Obama developed a reputation for being warm, engaging, humorous, and open. Such qualities made it easy for journalists to develop affirming and appealing storylines about how relatable the first lady was.

When the 2012 campaign began in earnest, Michelle Obama capitalized on her positive connection with members of the press. Her public activities, newsworthy by virtue of her standing as the first lady and because of her unusual frankness for someone in that position, gained lots of attention. Obama's media savvy showed when she effectively blended messages promoting her projects as first lady (e.g., *Let's Move!*) and advocating for her husband's reelection. By combining her social activism with her campaign efforts, Obama amassed a great deal of free media for the reelection campaign while staving off potential complaints that she was spending too much time barnstorming and not enough time fulfilling the responsibilities of a first lady. She also helped mitigate charges that she was politicizing what some think should be an apolitical position.

Throughout her time in the White House, Melania Trump developed a much more combative relationship with the press than most contemporary first ladies. Part of the problem stemmed from her husband's constant hostility toward mainstream media. As a candidate and as president, Donald Trump continually disputed the credibility of various journalists by calling widely respected news sources "fake news." He at times limited reporters' access to the White House and advocated for various degrees of censorship. In a few cases, he also made threats against the media and suggested that supporters inflict physical harm on newspeople. With such vitriolic rhetoric being spewed by her husband, it is not surprising that Melania Trump has not been able to establish the same kinds of reciprocal connections with members of the media that her predecessors did. In addition, she exacerbated the troublesome situation by taking her own antagonistic stance against the press. During her first two years in the White House, she rarely spoke to journalists directly, refused to distance herself from aggressive comments by her husband and his associates, and gave the impression she was trying to create tension between herself and the people covering her. Trump did not appear on entertainment programs and infrequently used her social media accounts. When she did make public appearances, she did not provide much substance for pundits to discuss. In short, she did little to positively influence the messaging surrounding her but seemed irritated that coverage of her was often disparaging.

Despite the fact that she has not yet cultivated an amiable relationship with reporters or endeavored to develop an appealing presence on social media, as a person in a newsworthy position, Trump could still use the power of the first lady pulpit if she chose to do so during the 2020 presidential campaign. In fact, her relative silence compared to previous first ladies might be helpful because the infrequency of her direct public remarks means that, when she does speak, she is bound to gain attention. If Trump decides to serve as an active advocate for her husband, she could start by developing a voice of her own. By strategically granting particular members of the media more access to her personally, not simply to her spokesperson, and by candidly answering questions that reveal more of her personality, Trump could display some independence and distinguish herself from her husband in a manner that could entice the public to regard her much more positively.

The support Melania Trump received for simple displays of autonomy (such as occasionally refusing to hold Donald's hand) indicates that voters would like her to be more of her own person and to accentuate her individuality. Doing so through particular media could help her appeal to specific audiences while establishing connections with the press. Appearing on morning television programs and daytime talk shows would allow the first lady to keep her comments directed toward topics related to home and family. Because her husband has been a rather polarizing president, queries about his policies and actions likely will arise. If this happens, she could choose to respond, or she could do as Barbara Bush and Laura Bush did for many years and politely decline to address the issue. If Melania Trump had a specific initiative or cause to promote when she granted interviews or visited television programs, she would have a ready subject to focus on or to redirect attention toward should there be inquiries about her husband's political maneuvering that she preferred not to answer. Many first ladies of the past have separated themselves from their husbands' political actions with relative ease. Laura Bush was particularly adept at doing so and maintained exceptionally high favorability ratings even as her husband's approval scores sank. Melania Trump could follow Bush's lead, but it would require actively developing her own independent public persona.

The advantages sitting first ladies enjoy during reelection campaigns move beyond simply having the experience of the first campaign and their time in the White House to inform their behaviors and strategies, as well as easier access to the media if they choose to utilize it. From a very practical perspective, the Office of the First Lady is a useful asset for a campaigning first lady. Possessing a staff of her own to help manage her time and devise communication strategies focused on maintaining and protecting her public image can be very beneficial for any woman who is tasked with fulfilling the nebulous duties of the first lady while advocating for her husband's reelection. With rare exceptions, spouses of presidential challengers tend not to have campaign personnel dedicated solely to their needs. In 2004, Teresa Heinz Kerry, the very wealthy wife of Democratic nominee John Kerry, did hire her own crew of campaign workers to help manage the various demands placed on a candidate's spouse, and she was pilloried for doing so. Pundits called it an ostentatious show of her wealth and self-importance, and opponents insinuated that Heinz Kerry was not up to serving as first lady if she could not survive the campaign without an entourage. The wives of presidents seeking reelection rarely confront such complaints although they do have formal additional help. Questions might occasionally be raised about the appropriate use of the Office of the First Lady when a presidential consort is an active campaigner, but because the boundaries of the first lady's responsibilities are unclear, such complaints are rarely sustained.

Because the first lady must continue to meet the expectations of her position while assisting with her husband's reelection efforts, her official staff cannot help but be tangentially involved in particular aspects of the campaign no matter what efforts are made to separate the campaign staff and the White House personnel. It would have been impossible for Michelle Obama to fully disconnect her actions as a campaigner and her functions as first lady. As mentioned above, many of her appearances to promote social causes included comments in support of her husband's reelection efforts, and many of her campaign messages referenced several of her initiatives as first lady. Obama's White House staff had to maintain her schedule, work in tandem with Secret Service personnel to assure that travel protocols were met, and manage the first lady's correspondence with the public. Each of these duties merged elements of the campaign and the expected daily actions of the White House matriarch.

Perhaps the most important and impactful aspect of Obama having a staff was the fact that there were people making sure the first lady, her interests, and her contributions to the nation were not disregarded as her husband sought a second term in office. Because she was already a highly active first lady and a very involved mother of school-aged daughters, when Michelle Obama again became a prominent campaign surrogate, it was like adding a third job to her list of occupations. Having employees to help her manage one of the three positions made it possible for Obama, one of only two mothers of young children to campaign as a first lady in the past several decades, to balance her multiple responsibilities.

The assistants in the East Wing ensured that the issues and projects Obama championed as first lady were not ignored or derailed as she supported her husband's campaign.

Melania Trump will need to decide how active she wants to be in the 2020 campaign relatively soon. If she maintains the docile approach she took in 2016, the merits of having a staff to support her needs will not be as great as with more active first lady campaigners. Trump could choose to concentrate on her responsibilities as a mother and first lady instead of hitting the campaign trail for the president. If this is the case, there will be little merging of East Wing and campaign scheduling functions, and the members of the Office of the First Lady will not need to help Trump balance her time between competing interests. However, if Trump decides to assume a more vocal role in her husband's reelection effort, her White House staff could be of tremendous use. They could work to prepare her by helping the first lady develop a more appealing public persona. Scheduling more speaking engagements for Trump and shaping a more concrete set of initiatives that connect the first lady more directly with the public would create potential bridges between Trump and voters. Rather than having a spokeswoman relay her remarks, Trump and her staff should craft comments that the first lady delivers herself. If there are concerns about her accent or her English skills, training and practice will help. Seeking assistance with her presentation skills would put Melania Trump in the company of Eleanor Roosevelt, who worked extensively with a speech coach before her husband ran for governor of New York. Additionally, the more the public gets used to hearing from the first lady, the less unusual her speaking style will seem. A communication specialist focused on shaping the first lady's messaging could serve Trump well both as first lady and as a prospective surrogate for her husband.

Heading into the 2012 election, Michelle Obama benefited from several of the same perks of being a sitting first lady that many of her predecessors enjoyed. She could summon substantial (and free) media attention almost at will, had a well-cultivated public persona, and managed a dedicated staff of her own. She had enhanced credibility based on the legitimacy that came with her position and her experience in the White House. In addition, Obama had been through a successful presidential campaign and did not have to expend energy navigating a months-long primary race. Having learned from her own gaffes and challenges in 2008, Obama was able to approach the reelection effort with the confidence of a seasoned campaigner. She also maintained higher favorability ratings than her husband for most of her time in the public eye. Therefore, it was no surprise that she figured prominently in Barack Obama's bid to secure a second term in office. Her second presidential race was not the same as her first, but her overall participation was quite familiar.

Melania Trump could choose to avail herself of many of the assets available to her as a first lady supporting her husband's reelection campaign. She could look to history for examples of reticent spouses who became more effective surrogates during a subsequent campaign and model herself after women such as Barbara and Laura Bush. Both of the Bush first ladies initially refused to share their political perspectives, with Barbara famously deferring to her husband in public and Laura adroitly changing the subject whenever controversial topics arose. Yet, both women became noticeably more visible and assertive while campaigning as first lady. Barbara Bush gave her opinion on abortion, chastised Republican operatives for ugly campaign tactics, and redefined the concept of "family" in the GOP effort to protect family values. Laura Bush talked more openly about women's rights, framed military action in terms of its impact on families, and addressed the ways the economy impacted women who owned small businesses. Both women leveraged their likeability to help their husbands, but neither woman lost any ground for expressing herself. Melania Trump has the potential to enhance public perceptions of her as a first lady and perhaps help her husband win over particular kinds of voters, but this will require more frequent interactions with the citizenry.

DISADVANTAGES OF CAMPAIGNING AS FIRST LADY

Even though women whose husbands are running for reelection have many advantages over challengers' spouses, there are also some downsides to campaigning while residing in the White House. Much like incumbent presidents, sitting first ladies have a record of public activity that can be used against them. In addition, some of the elements that might be considered positive, such as the ability to garner media attention and having an established public persona, can also become problematic for first ladies as campaign surrogates. Any president's spouse who chooses to actively advocate for her husband to retain the Oval Office must understand and effectively navigate the potential pitfalls that come along with that decision.

Contemporary presidential spouses have been markedly more publicly engaged than their earlier counterparts, both as White House matriarchs and as surrogate electioneers. The public now expects to see and hear from the first lady on a relatively regular basis. The increased pressure for public action means that by the time her husband's second campaign begins in earnest, the first lady has had plenty of opportunities to develop her own record as a public servant. For many first ladies, their behaviors in the public eye provide a favorable foundation for their efforts as campaigners, but for others, awkward moments create challenges. Such difficulties might stem specifically from their time as first lady or from missteps during the previous campaign.

Perhaps one of the best examples of a modern first lady who encountered significant troubles during her husband's reelection bid because of her own public record was Hillary Clinton during the 1996 race. Clinton's controversial image had roots that not only ran back to her many purported gaffes during the 1992 campaign but also to her somewhat tumultuous history as the first lady of Arkansas. When Bill Clinton lost his 1980 race for a second term as the governor of Arkansas, pundits were quick to blame Hillary Clinton for his defeat by claiming her ostensibly nontraditional demeanor had turned voters away from her husband. She was critiqued for her appearance, her professional ambition, and her decision to use her maiden name of Rodham. The couple made adjustments to their outward image, and Bill won several subsequent terms as governor, but Hillary's persona never fully recovered.

During the 1992 campaign, Hillary Clinton was lambasted for being a so-called modern woman and was accused of having disdain for women with more conventional perspectives. One of the most notorious moments occurred when Clinton was asked to defend her decision to pursue a career. Although she actually professed support for women's ability to make whatever choices they wanted, reporters highlighted a truncated part of the statement in which Clinton dismissively said, "I suppose I could have stayed home, baked cookies and held teas."[1] Several members of the media argued this comment was an indication of her disregard for homemakers. After encountering substantial backlash, Clinton tried to rehabilitate her image by accentuating her own experiences as a home-maker and mother, but the press and the public doubted the sincerity of her presumed newfound focus on domesticity. Her attempted im-age adjustment was further questioned when Clinton led attempts at national health care reform shortly after her husband was inaugurated. Opponents claimed her assumption of such a consequential role was an indication of her overly ambitious nature and that it ran counter to the docile mother-figure image she tried to project at the end of the 1992 campaign. After her legislative efforts failed, Clinton's public persona suffered additional setbacks. She was unable to effectively portray herself as either a traditional woman or a competent political operative.

Clinton's record haunted her a great deal during the 1996 race. The "bake cookies" clip and the various misrepresentations of it were re-played numerous times. Pundits and politicos also continually revived complaints about her unsuccessful leadership regarding health care re-form. In addition, commentators took aim at the first lady for her role in several White House scandals. As a result, Hillary Clinton's overall par-ticipation in her husband's 1996 campaign was considerably more muted that it had been in 1992. She focused primarily on fund-raising, and when she did give interviews or speak on her husband's behalf, Clinton tended to underscore her supportiveness of her husband and her responsibilities as a mother. She appeared more frequently with her daughter than she had during the previous election and avoided making comments of a controversial nature. Clinton tried to learn from her experiences during the first campaign and her time in the White House, but the press and her political opponents used her extensive public activity against her. The criticisms of Clinton did not adversely affect her husband's reelec-tion effort, but her problematic public image did shadow her throughout her time in politics.

Michelle Obama seemed to negotiate the downside of having a re-cord of public behavior much more effectively than Hillary Clinton did. There were criticisms of Obama throughout her first few years as first lady, but she largely avoided stirring controversy after a couple of gaffes during the 2008 campaign. Opponents attempted to revive critiques about the first lady's purported lack of patriotism by dredging up old arguments about an essay she had written as a Princeton undergraduate, but her extensive work on behalf of military families countered many of the objections that had been previously leveled against her. Conservative commentators also tried to resuscitate concerns about Obama not fitting the mold of a traditional first lady by complaining about her physique, her wardrobe, and the way she behaved in public. They pointed to the times she went sleeveless, wore shorts on vacation, and did push-ups on television to claim that she was not demure enough to continue as the White House matriarch. Obama's supporters countered these critiques by asserting that the first lady was a more compelling and relatable representation of American womanhood than many of her predecessors. By largely ignoring the old criticisms, Obama managed to render most of them a nonissue in the 2012 campaign.

Despite the fact that the majority of attempts to discredit Michelle Obama were grounded in complaints that had emerged in 2008, her efforts to help end childhood obesity provided new grounds for attack. The most vexing argument that grew out of Obama's *Let's Move!* campaign was that the first lady was advocating for the development of a so-called nanny state in which the government dictated the daily behaviors of citizens. Politicos claimed that Obama's work to make school lunches more nutritious and to encourage kids to exercise were indicative of her desire to limit Americans' freedoms, including impinging on a person's right to be unhealthy. The more extreme pundits tried to dissolve some of the positive regard the public had for Obama by asserting that the first lady was trying to promote and normalize socialism through her programs.

Michelle Obama effectively negotiated the potential pitfalls of an existing record by attempting to behave in an appropriate and acceptable manner for a first lady throughout her time in the White House. By keeping much of her influence over her husband and his policies private, publicly championing so-called feminine causes like children's health and supporting military families, and maintaining a relatable image as a working mom, Obama built a base of approval that was difficult for opponents to erode during the election and that was easy for her to build on as a campaigner. Giving speeches at events she headlined, Obama underscored her independence while demonstrating her loyalty to her husband. She expressed her own opinions, most of which aligned with her husband's perspectives, in a manner that spotlighted her maternal standing and highlighted her special experiences living in the White House. In this way, Obama confirmed her persona as an ordinary woman in an extraordinary position. She encouraged many American women of various races and ethnicities to relate to her on a personal level and to see themselves in her representations of womanhood, making her both a respected first lady and an effective campaigner.

For the 2020 campaign, Melania Trump will confront more problems regarding her established record than Michelle Obama did. Although her public actions and supposed gaffes were not as diverse, entrenched, or enduring as those attributed to Hillary Clinton, Melania Trump's many ostensible missteps and her connection to various scandals (see chapter 4) increase the difficulties she will encounter if she chooses to campaign actively for her husband. It is likely that her nude photos will once again be part of the campaign against her husband, particularly if the president is significantly challenged during the Republican nomination (most incumbents have few serious primary opponents, but Donald Trump's controversial nature could invite party in-fighting).

If Melania Trump decides to be more vocal in 2020 than she was in 2016, she will confront questions about the authorship of her messaging. Should she once again address the RNC, Trump's speech will be carefully dissected and compared to addresses by past first ladies, particularly those by Michelle Obama. Even if Trump's new RNC speech does not contain plagiarized passages, there will certainly be a slew of reports reminding audiences of the scandal caused by her 2016 address. News sources will play side-by-side clips of Obama's 2008 address and Trump's 2016 speech numerous times leading up to the convention, regardless of whether or not Trump gives another speech, and the past indiscretion will be described online and on television countless times. Any concerns about the origination of Trump's campaign orations will reignite arguments about Trump's honesty and reopen debates about her intellectual ability. Because of the way Trump handled the 2016 incident, and because the press and the public seem eager to catch the first lady committing similar bad acts, it will be impossible for Melania Trump to avoid such efforts to impugn her credibility. However, she could mitigate the potential problems associated with this aspect of her past behavior by hiring a cautious, experienced speechwriter. She should not claim credit for composing her own speeches but should work closely with a seasoned politico who can help her develop a voice of her own and who can reframe the themes commonly found in first ladies' campaign speeches in ways that are unique to Trump.

Melania Trump could also simply choose to avoid participating in her husband's reelection campaign altogether. She could explain her lack of involvement by repeating her previous statements about not being interested in political affairs and underscoring her preference for focusing on her duties as a mother. Such an approach would have the advantage of reinforcing her embrace of traditional femininity by highlighting her maternal drive and her deferential nature. However, refusing to publicly endorse her husband will not prevent stories from being written about the alleged plagiarism incident from the previous cycle and could provoke speculation about her actual support for Donald. Additionally, because of the numerous reports about the degree of her rumored disappointment when her husband won in 2016, refusing to actively participate in a reelection campaign, no matter her reason, could revive arguments about Trump's reluctance to serve as the first lady. In 2020, Melania Trump will not be able to fully escape the difficulties created by her past public actions, but she might be able to lessen their impact if she is willing to expand her staff and overcome her own reticence to become a more forceful campaigner.

First ladies who act as political surrogates also face distinct disadvantages based on the perpetual media attention they receive. Earlier in this chapter, the relationship a president's spouse has with the press was identified as a potential advantage in a reelection campaign, and it certainly can be a significant asset. Still, the constant coverage a first lady encounters can also be detrimental to her efforts as a campaign surrogate. Problems can arise when there is little substance available to discuss. In such situations journalists begin speculating rather than reporting. The ambiguity of the first lady role invites pundits to insert their own idiosyncratic interpretations of the job or of womanhood into their assessments of first lady campaigners.

The expansion of the media environment in the late twentieth century created the 24/7 news cycle and changed what it means for something to be newsworthy. Presidential spouses have been the focus of media attention for many decades, but as more information outlets have emerged, coverage of first ladies has broadened. Almost any public activity by a first lady is now widely reported, interpreted, and judged. Modern first ladies cannot escape the endless evaluations of them by friends and foes alike, and the advent of social media has widened the number of commentators further. Members of the media try to interpret a first lady's acts in terms of their impact on politics, on social mores, or, particularly during reelection campaigns, on her husband's potential success or failure. The wives of incumbent presidents experience additional attention during a presidential campaign because, as reporters write pieces about key characters in the election, first ladies are more accessible than challengers' consorts, their established personas offer ready-made storylines that require less contextual explication, there is a wealth of existing video footage of them, and the spouses' dual status as public servants and political advocates creates potential points of tension that can be sensationalized.

Michelle Obama generally negotiated the downside of the media's insatiable desire for information about her by being relatively active throughout the 2012 campaign. Her willingness to grant journalists access to her events as first lady and as a surrogate campaigner encouraged reporters to assume that her transparency was a sign of trustworthiness, so they mostly treated her as someone with nothing to hide. In addition, the largely positive relationship she developed with the mainstream media led to fewer antagonistic stories about her. However, alternative online news sources were significantly more varied in their assessments and treatment of the first lady. Because many niche online outlets cater to very specific audiences with particular political and social points of view, sites with ultra-right-wing readers tended to berate Obama for pretty much every action she took. Those types of sources offered commentaries about the first lady that included many clear attacks on her as a woman and as an African American (see chapter 4), and they propagated unfounded rumors about her. Obama, her staffers, and other members of her husband's reelection campaign largely ignored the reports from such sources and the mainstream press dismissed the so-called fringe sites as inconsequential outlets with small audiences. While their impact was marginal in 2012, by the next election cycle they began to wield considerable influence with substantial blocks of the voting public.

One of the most effective strategies Michelle Obama used to manage adversarial coverage was to continually focus on fulfilling her duties as first lady while advocating on behalf of her husband. Because she balanced between promoting her husband and championing her own causes, Obama was able to successfully demonstrate her competence and compassion while giving journalists a lot to report on. Her level of activity meant that more time was spent chronicling her activities than speculating about her motives. She provided many useful quotations for writers to include in their stories, giving herself a voice in articles about her. She occasionally relied on a spokesperson, but she usually gave statements herself, either to members of the media or to the public through various social media outlets. By offering the media a wealth of substantive content to cover, Obama helped direct the attention paid to her and reduced commentators' need to conjecture about her. This is not to say that pundits did not verbalize their own opinions about her as a person, as a first lady, and as a campaigner, but Obama's accessibility and candor decreased the need to guess about her thoughts and actions.

During her first couple of years as the first lady, Melania Trump experienced firsthand the downside of a highly attentive media. She was critiqued for everything from her choice of footwear to the title of her signature initiative. Her apparent frustration with reporters became evident as she engaged in behavior that antagonized the press and tangentially disrespected the public, like when she wore the "I REALLY DON'T CARE, DO U?" jacket (see chapter 4). In addition, Trump's relative inaccessibility and tendency to disseminate comments primarily through her spokesperson created a gulf between the first lady, the news media, and the public. Without remedying the situation, Trump could encounter further adverse coverage during her husband's reelection campaign.

To lessen the challenges that come along with the extensive media attention she attracts, Trump should work on developing a better rapport with the public by using the news media as an ally and by engaging more directly through various social media outlets. Using a representative to make occasional comments is fine, but Trump needs to be more deliberate about when she should address a matter personally. For important issues, such as the separation of families at the border, Trump should be the one making statements about her own perspectives. Speaking for herself would win her public favor and would give pundits less of an opportunity to chastise her for purportedly hiding behind her spokesperson. In a few instances, Trump has gained respect from many people for exhibiting some independence by contradicting her husband through comments her staff has made on her behalf. She could enhance these positive effects if she were to make some of the remarks herself, taking her own stand and showing her character. Reaching out to audiences would allow Trump to control some of her own messaging and would give observers more substantive material on which to base their analysis of her personality and points of view. Although it would be extremely hard for Trump to turn all media coverage to her advantage, she could certainly decrease the potential negative impact of it by taking better command of her image and making more strategic communication decisions.

In much the same way that attention from the media can either be an advantage or a disadvantage for an incumbent first lady during a reelection campaign, her established persona can also become either an asset or a liability. In most cases, it has been beneficial for a first lady to have a well-cultivated public image regardless of whether the portrayal was positive or negative. On the affirming end of the spectrum, Barbara Bush was able to campaign quite effectively because her decade-long depiction as an amiable grandmother encouraged voters to interpret her actions as well-meaning even when they were quite aggressive (like when she called Geraldine Ferraro something that "rhymes with rich"[2]) or more political (such as when she shared her opinion on abortion) than the public had come to expect from the gregarious but usually deferential woman. On the less favorable side, Nancy Reagan was known for having a fierce will to protect her husband, so it was no surprise when she appeared as a feisty defender of Ronald during the 1984 campaign. Staffers and members of the media dismissed her occasional over-the-top comments as "Nancy being Nancy."[3] In both cases, a well-developed persona provided a lens through which the press and public could interpret the women and their actions. When a president's spouse does not form such a fixed image, her presumed unpredictability usually results in much less sympathetic treatment. Hillary Clinton's attempts to morph between an independent modern woman and a traditional homemaker caused her significant trouble throughout her public life.

Michelle Obama had an exceptionally stable persona that emphasized her embrace of conventional ideals of femininity. Although she was an intelligent and accomplished woman who had built a successful career, Obama's outward image instead highlighted her roles as a wife and especially as a mother. The decision to spotlight her domesticity during the 2008 campaign was both strategic and sincere. Obama had been a very active working mother and had supported her husband's political ambitions well before his presidential bid began, so those aspects of her public face were genuine. However, downplaying her professional accomplishments and underscoring her dutifulness to her family was a way of building a relatable image that dissolved some perceived distance between Obama and past first ladies as well as between Obama and women voters.

The image Obama built in 2008 made her a well-liked representative of American womanhood, shielded her from the kinds of criticism Hillary Clinton encountered in 1992 (and again in 1996), and gave her a political voice by couching her interests in terms of a concerned mother. It was a valuable but limited self-depiction. By grounding her own credibility in the fact of her maternity, Obama discounted the wealth of other experiences that made her an interesting and important person. Even though she made the case for other women to be independent political actors, her own authority always stemmed from her relationships with others. Obama's uniqueness, particularly with respect to her race but also based on many other aspects of her life and personality, made this type of self-representation necessary so she would not be viewed as a liability to her husband and his political aspirations. Once this maternal image was set, recalibrating it to include more of Obama's less conventional characteristics would have been very difficult. Therefore, in 2012,

Obama doubled down on her "everymom" persona and cast herself as the "mom-in-chief."

Michelle Obama benefited from her mother-focused depiction in 2012 in several ways. The portrayal provided a consistent lens through which people could view her and her actions. As she advocated for her husband, she made a case for his reelection that mothers across the nation could relate to. In addition, she was shielded from claims that her campaign activity was too assertive because she was promoting her husband instead of herself. The depiction also helped buttress the dedication of her base supporters. In particular, Obama helped secure votes from working mothers and stay-at-home moms who felt the first lady represented them and their interests. Furthermore, Obama presented herself as understanding average American women and their experiences in a way that Ann Romney, the Republican nominee's wife and a dedicated but extremely wealthy housewife, did not. Despite the fact that Obama's life had actually been rather extraordinary, her persona created a perception that she was similar to most women and that she knew what it was like to struggle in various ways. Michelle Obama's outward persona was familiar and widely applauded; thus, it was a decided advantage during the 2012 campaign.

Melania Trump's public image throughout the 2016 election and her first couple of years in the White House was not particularly well developed. Unlike Michelle Obama, whose public image was quite specific—a working mother who sacrificed a successful career to support her husband and care for her daughters—Trump's most accentuated attribute was her relative silence. During her time in the White House, analysts tried to create a more detailed understanding of the first lady by speculating about some of her actions. A few sympathetic politicos called her refusal to hold her husband's hand an act of defiant independence and claimed statements released through her spokesperson denouncing family separations at the border and praising LeBron James for opening a school for at-risk children were attempts to separate herself from her husband. They also labeled her disappearance from the public eye at the height of a sex scandal involving her husband a show of self-preservation. Still, these characterizations were widely dismissed as endeavors from outsiders to create a more palatable image of Trump than she herself actually offered.

Due to her quiescence and her relative lack of visibility, Melania Trump's persona became that of a deferential cipher. This fairly insubstantial image was problematic for the first lady because it provided little insight into her motivations and did not guide interpretations of her behaviors in the way that past first ladies' personas did. The uncertainty surrounding Trump's assumed perspectives left plenty of opportunity for reporters and pundits to speculate about her. Her failure to distinguish herself from her husband led most commentators to interpret her as a simple extension of Donald, and the polarizing nature of her husband and his actions meant most conjecture about Melania Trump was negative. However, there is still some potential for the first lady to cultivate a more vocal and engaged persona that could positively impact both her ability to advocate for her husband and her overall legacy as the first lady. To do so, she should take some cues from Laura Bush.

During the 2000 presidential campaign, Laura Bush was portrayed as a relatively silent but steadfast part of her husband's bid for the Oval Office. She was not a particularly vocal surrogate, but when she did speak she was charming, deferential, and unwavering in her support for George W. Bush. In 2004, the once purportedly reserved woman was appearing solo on television and in campaign ads. She expressed her own opinion more often and, although still charming and deferential, she adopted a more assertive tone. Journalists contended that from one presidential campaign to the next, Laura Bush had evolved from a "cool Marian the Librarian . . . into a hot Mary Matalin."[4] Bush shifted her public image, but her alterations were gradual and remained within the realm of her originally developed persona as a dedicated proponent of her husband. Because her self-depiction changed fairly slowly, Bush was credited with having experienced a political awakening during her time in the White House. She was not accused of altering her persona as part of a political ploy the way Clinton was.

Melania Trump could learn from Laura Bush's transformation and modify her own self-depiction by being strategic about her activities, her public statements, and her use of the media. Her decision to visit the housing centers for children who'd been separated from their families at the border was a good first step, but she sabotaged the move with her choice of attire (see chapter 3). Her expression of compassion and concern was much like Laura Bush's meeting with women from the Middle East. For Bush, the gathering was part of a new initiative she'd adopted regarding the promotion of women's rights around the world. For Trump, the visit to the detention center could have been the start of a new and more concrete effort to aid immigrant children. She could have used her status as a naturalized citizen to build her credibility and to draw attention to a different facet of the debate on immigration reform. Taking such a stance might have been viewed as a challenge to her husband, but she could have finessed the discussion (as Laura Bush did with women's rights) to make the topic appear less about politics and more about showing sympathy for the young. Instead, Trump loosely tied her trips to her amorphous and ill-defined *Be Best* campaign.

There are opportunities for Melania Trump to redefine her image by selecting more tangible and substantial causes to champion and engaging in more media-friendly events that would showcase her social advocacy. Rather than thinking about photo-ops, she and her staff need to plan interactive activities where she is able to really demonstrate her concern for children and give the press something to cover that extends beyond a picture or two and a brief statement by a media liaison. Trump needs to be more deliberate about the image she wants to portray of herself—it should be something that is consistent with her history and is not a jarring shift from her existing image—and then sponsor and attend events that support that persona. As long as the self-presentation is a genuine reflection of some aspect of her personality, there is a distinct possibility that Melania Trump can establish her own identity and use it both to assist in her husband's reelection efforts and to curate a more effective legacy for herself as the first lady.

The disadvantages of campaigning while first lady are closely tied to the advantages of being in that position during a reelection bid. Whether a particular element such as media attention or a public image becomes an asset or a liability largely depends on the first lady's behaviors during the first campaign and her first couple of years as the White House matron. For Michelle Obama, the various potential drawbacks were limited because of her friendly relationship with the media and her adroitly constructed and managed public persona. Melania Trump, on the other hand, did not negotiate the 2016 campaign or her first several months in the East Wing in nearly as successful a manner. Her contentious relationship with the press and less concretely defined persona could cause difficulties for her as she continues in the job and if she decides to campaign vigorously on behalf of her husband in 2020. Still, as many of the suggestions above demonstrate, if she makes some strategic efforts to rehabilitate her image, Trump can become a more powerful and engaging first lady and a more consequential electioneer.

Presidents' spouses can be some of the most effective surrogates during a reelection campaign. Because the first ladyship is purported to be apolitical, the person in the role can more readily attempt to build her appeal across partisan lines than other political operatives. In addition, first ladies tend to establish a better rapport with the public at large and frequently have higher favorability ratings than their husbands because much of their public activity revolves around engaging in social advocacy and showing compassion for citizens in various types of need. As White House matriarchs, these women are also assumed to have special, intimate knowledge about the president; therefore, they are credible in ways other surrogates are not. However, campaigning as first lady is not without its drawbacks, and all presidents' mates who engage in their husbands' reelection efforts must work to accentuate the benefits of electioneering from the East Wing while mitigating the disadvantages. As each first lady decides whether and how she participates in a presidential campaign, she impacts expectations for the helpmates that succeed her.

Michelle Obama set pretty high standards as a campaigner, particularly when she did so from the White House. She was a relatively outgoing first lady who did not shun media attention, who stayed effectively on message while avoiding the appearance of being controlled by staffers, and who consistently reinforced a masterfully developed public persona that invited a wide range of voters to connect with her on a personal level. Her candor was appealing to many citizens, and her positive relationship with most mainstream media outlets meant that much of the coverage of her and her campaign efforts was favorable. Obama's accessibility and frankness cultivated an expectation that future first ladies be equally outgoing and transparent. The fact that she was well regarded and earned some of the highest favorability ratings among modern first ladies makes Obama a campaigning first lady others should want to model themselves after.

Melania Trump had a tough act to follow both as a campaigner in 2016 and as the first lady of the United States. Her interest in and style of campaigning was dramatically different from that of her immediate predecessor. Most observers would argue that, although it did not seem to hinder her husband's success, Melania Trump's 2016 mode of election-eering was not particularly compelling. Still, as the first lady, she has the potential to be a positive force in her husband's 2020 campaign. Unlike Obama, who had a favorable image to build on and amplify, Trump needs to rehabilitate her persona if she is interested in expanding her appeal to voters. If she wishes to create a more positive image for herself, Trump could accentuate her own individuality by speaking on her own behalf, expressing her own interests and perspectives, and showing voters the sense of humor she has been rumored to display in private settings. Of course, whether she becomes an active participant in the 2020 campaign will only partially be her decision. It will also depend on her husband and his advisers. However, because of the power of the first lady pulpit, Melania Trump could resolve to become a more effective and admired first lady by adapting some of her communicative tendencies, regardless of her role in the president's reelection bid.

If the first lady decides not to be an active part of Donald Trump's efforts to retain the Oval Office, she could actually broaden opportunities for future presidents' spouses. Each first lady has some flexibility in defining the position, but most are inclined to fulfill the expectations established by those who came before them. By breaking with the tradition of presidential mates actively endorsing and promoting their spouses in reelection campaigns, Melania Trump might open a space for future presidents' mates to choose to be less politically involved if that is what they wish. Despite the fact that it might appear to be a regressive step back to the days of female disempowerment, Trump could afford future presidential spouses more options for setting the parameters of how they approach the unpaid and ill-defined role of first lady.

Afterword

Contrasting Michelle Obama and Melania Trump

THE DESIRE TO COMPARE FIRST LADIES WITH THEIR PREDECES-
sors and successors is an understandable one. The women who have
filled this undefined role have been a mix of traditional and unconventional individuals, all of whom had to find a way to make the position
their own while being burdened by the expectations society and previous presidential consorts placed on them. Contrasting those who have
served as the White House matron provides some insights into various
aspects of the individuals who have done the job (e.g., Michelle Obama's
particular rhetorical savvy appealing to multiple diverse audiences) and
the job itself (e.g., the complex nature of some of the uncodified duties
and requirements, and the constant partisanship that colors evaluations
of presidential helpmates). However, as explained earlier, most side-by-
side analyses of presidential spouses are limited by the ways observers interpret the women and the functions of the first ladyship (see the
introduction).

This book has taken a broad-based view of Michelle Obama and Melania Trump as candidates' spouses, wives of presidents-elect, and first
ladies by using past presidential helpmates to contextualize the women's
actions and inform the assessment of them. Because it is focused on
the public images of Obama and Trump, this book offers a perspective
distinct from one examining the daily lives of the women or presenting

a behind-the-scenes peek into the modern White House. After this volume's in-depth review of the ways Obama and Trump approached the public aspects of being a political wife, it is important to take a few pages to consider the reasons why the two women are judged so differently by the public at large and whether there is a fundamental lack of fairness that accompanies the appraisals of these first ladies.

There is no question that the general public has viewed Michelle Obama and Melania Trump in antithetical ways since they were both first-time candidates' wives. Obama has routinely scored on the higher end of most favorability ratings in relation to other candidates' spouses and first ladies, whereas Trump has frequently landed on the lower end of the scale. Obama's polling data throughout her time in the White House averaged at or above 65 percent positive. For Trump, rising above 50 percent for the first time eleven months into her first ladyship was hailed as a remarkable achievement. Since 1969, when opinion polls about first ladies started regularly being taken, the lowest recorded mark before Trump was Betty Ford's initial score of 50 percent positive (which increased to 71 percent by the next year).[1] Melania Trump has had higher ratings than her husband but still ranks among the least liked of all modern first ladies—and her low score is accentuated by the fact that Melania Trump succeeded the well-regarded Michelle Obama. Although the numbers are pretty clear, pitting the two women against one another is a troublesome (though common) practice for a number of reasons.

The amorphous nature of the first ladyship makes a head-to-head analysis of Michelle Obama and Melania Trump problematic. Most political positions have specific duties and particular authority assigned them. This makes discerning how competently a person fulfills his or her responsibilities relatively straightforward and allows for stable points of analysis between those who have held the job. Even if people prioritize different aspects of the post, the standards for effectiveness are reasonably consistent. Yet, because the first ladyship is not constitutionally mandated and lacks a clearly delineated set of expectations, there are no set standards for evaluating whether a person is fit for the role and how satisfactorily someone performs it. In fact, the only requirement for becoming first lady is being married to the person who assumes the presidency (and in the case of widower or bachelor presidents, even marriage was not necessary). The ambiguity surrounding the first ladyship opens anyone vying for or taking on the enterprise to all sorts of founded and unfounded critiques. Still, because the presidential helpmate is treated as a formally established position with fixed obligations, people presume that anyone who takes on this challenge is adequately and equally qualified to serve as the first lady. While technically true (it is impossible not to meet nonexistent standards), in reality, every woman who has been a first lady has had significantly different experiences, skill sets, and bases of knowledge.

When considering Michelle Obama and Melania Trump, it is essential to remember that though the women had many similarities (see the introduction), they were also distinct individuals with different backgrounds and sets of expertise that informed the ways they approached public life. In addition, the contexts for their respective first ladyships influenced the ways each enacted the nebulous role. In order to more fully understand why the two women were viewed in such divergent manners, it is useful to briefly revisit their histories with an eye toward how their pre–White House lives prepared them (or failed to do so) for life as the president's mate.

The first point to account for is the way the women's professions resulted in their different competencies and sensibilities. Although both women pursued competitive careers, Michelle Obama as an attorney and public relations professional and Melania Trump as a model, the valued elements of their occupations were quite different. Obama had a particularly other-centric professional life. Her work as a lawyer required that she understand how to manage clients' needs; build arguments that people would find compelling; and negotiate with opponents, bosses, and judges. When Obama switched jobs and began working in the public sector, she spent a great deal of time interacting with a variety of people and showing concern for the well-being of an assortment of individuals, factions, and communities. At the University of Chicago Hospitals, her work in community and external affairs required that she develop exceptional communicative skills while she served as a liaison between the hospital and the many publics it served. Obama's work prepared her to engage effectively with others on an individual and group basis and honed her public speaking abilities.

For Melania Trump, the prized characteristics for her job were her appearance and her ability to follow directions. She was not often required to speak publicly, and when she did, she was not expected to be particularly eloquent. Her ability to attract attention or hold an audience's interest was based on her looks and on her willingness to defer to the commands of others (e.g., photographers, designers, and fashion directors). She had to be strategic about the choices she made regarding her career, but her daily work life had little to do with making decisions that impacted others or with persuading members of the public through verbal interactions.

Based on the career tracks of Michelle Obama and Melania Trump, Obama should be the more verbally skillful and accessible of the two. Obama's years of experience working to win over audiences of various types and sizes prepared her for the numerous duties of a candidate's wife and a first lady. She knew how to adapt to her audience without coming across as inauthentic. Meanwhile, Trump's professional life prepared her to serve more as a visual adornment than a responsive, self-directed agent. It makes sense that she acted model-like during her days on the campaign trail and was silent rather than expressive. When she did speak, Trump was frequently criticized for her accent, her overly rehearsed delivery, and her lack of originality. Even though not all models are deferential and not all Ivy League–trained lawyers are personable, in the cases of Melania Trump and Michelle Obama, the women's occupational backgrounds clearly impacted the ways each approached life as a political spouse.

A second observation stemming from a direct comparison between Michelle Obama and Melania Trump is that there is an expectation that all presidential spouses must become public figures and public servants because of their marital connection to the president. First ladies are pressured to abandon their careers, relocate their families, and build social agendas that the public will find appealing and appropriate for a president's spouse. Because she holds a position that is unelected and not appointed, most people do not want the first lady to extend her influence beyond a particular, but unstated, realm. Even though the first lady is not paid, the role has no officially defined responsibilities, and the post is dependent on someone else's political ambition, modern presidents'

spouses are not permitted to decline the responsibilities of the first ladyship and live a private life while their husbands lead the nation. Moreover, there is a presumption that modern presidential consorts desire
the status and attention that comes along with life in the White House.

Most contemporary presidential spouses have been political mates
for a long time before their husbands secured the presidency. Because
they have served as supportive consorts for many years, often improving
their own public image and enhancing their status as their mates moved
up the political ladder, it is easy to understand why the public might
believe that candidates' wives are eager to become the White House
matriarch. In 2008, Michelle Obama had been through multiple local-
and state-level contests with her husband. She was by his side at the 2004
Democratic National Convention when he delivered the address that
started speculation about a presidential bid, and stories surfaced early
about Michelle Obama's involvement as her husband's adviser. By the
time the 2008 campaign started in earnest, Obama had overcome her
initial ambivalence about her husband's campaign and encouraged his
efforts. Her active engagement with the press and the public gave the
impression she was enthusiastic about becoming the first lady. Obama
did lament the restrictive nature of life in the White House, yet no one
publicly doubted that she was genuinely interested in overseeing the East
Wing. The same was not true of her successor.

Melania Trump had the least experience as a political spouse of any
woman who has become first lady in several decades. Her husband's first
official run for any office was for the presidency in 2016. There were no
previous campaigns for a senate or congressional seat for her to endure or
learn from. Her husband was never a political appointee or public servant
in any capacity. His public life revolved around his status as a celebrity
businessman and reality television personality. Melania Trump was a
minor celebrity partially because of her days as a model, but primarily
due to her marriage to the boisterous Donald Trump. Because her husband's fame was built largely on an image of brashness and braggadocio,
Melania Trump was not encouraged to build an outward persona that
emphasized her regard for others the way most political spouses are.
Instead, she was widely viewed derogatorily as a "trophy wife" whose
primary duties were to look good and add to her husband's perceived

virility. Trump was not nearly as prepared to be a president's spouse as most of her predecessors were; still, she was routinely compared with women who had spent years, if not decades, of their lives negotiating the expectations placed on the mates of politically ambitious men.

By most accounts, Trump did not foresee that her life would take such a turn and place her in the position of having to be a public servant. She was not elected to an office, yet she was unable to decline to serve as the presidential helpmate. She was pressured by social and political conventions to assume a post she had no training for and might not have wanted. With little guidance and no sustained history of social advocacy, she was compelled to create appropriate and actionable initiatives she could champion. Given her lack of experience, it is not surprising that Melania Trump is often found wanting when measured against both the ever-changing requirements of the role and the more seasoned women who managed the East Wing before her.

The third issue highlighted by the one-to-one assessments of Michelle Obama and Melania Trump is associated with both the first and the second. It is the presumption that first ladies be likeable and relatable. There is a widespread notion that the person linked most intimately to the nation's leader, particularly if a woman, be a compassionate and outgoing person with the ability and desire to build bonds with large facets of the citizenry. Creating connections with a constituency is usually achieved through the successful development of an inviting public persona, by conveying personal stories that highlight shared interests, and by discussing issues in a manner that illustrates a clear understanding of others' experiences. Many modern first ladies hone their ability to build bonds with others during their early days as political spouses or through their education and professional training.

The career-based differences in the skill sets Michelle Obama and Melania Trump established before each became the first lady substantially impacted how effectively each woman was able to build associations with groups of citizens. Michelle Obama benefited from a lifetime of experience sharpening her communication skills and learning to identify with others. Many aspects of her education were geared toward understanding diversity and finding ways of bridging gaps between herself and others and between different groups of people. Her professional endeavors required that she be empathetic, adroitly find common ground between various stakeholders, and relate to people on a personal level. She also needed to think strategically and balance between short-term gains and long-term goals. All of these skills helped Obama as she campaigned for her husband and served as a likeable and generally respected first lady.

Melania Trump's ability to appeal to voters in ways other than through her visual attractiveness was limited because of her past experiences. Her pre–White House life required that she be desirable rather than likeable. Professionally, she had to be sufficiently cooperative and photogenic to secure jobs as a model. Personally, she needed to be captivating enough to capture and retain the romantic interest of Donald Trump. After she became a minor celebrity by marrying Donald Trump, Melania's life became a bit more public but not necessarily more focused on others (with the notable exception of her attentiveness to her son). She engaged in some philanthropic work, but it required little public speaking and did not mandate that she build a personal rapport with broad audiences. As a businesswoman, Trump made several media appearances, but her efforts were geared toward promoting her products, not necessarily getting viewers to know her personally. Melania Trump never really had to build personal associations with diverse people before she became the first lady, something the more esteemed presidential spouses accomplished with apparent ease.

Throughout this book, the importance of the public personas Obama and Trump developed has been discussed numerous times. Still, because the images each promulgated had such influence over how the public perceived the women and their ability to build meaningful connections with others, they bear revisiting once more. Michelle Obama crafted an outward persona that was concrete and coherent. During the 2008 campaign, she cultivated an "everymom" image that amplified aspects of the popular soccer mom trope (a 1990s conceptualization of the working suburban mother whose primary concern was her family). Although the category itself was limited and did not actually depict the complexities of Obama's life, it was a well-known political archetype that gave audience members an easy and positive lens through which to view and relate to the eventual first lady. The image accounted for Obama's professional success without emphasizing it, made motherhood a central aspect of her identity, and encouraged mothers of all sorts to perceive the first lady as someone who had similar experiences and interests as they had. Obama reinforced this image by talking frankly about her background as a mother and wife and sharing anecdotes that illustrated the supposedly ordinary nature of her family life. In this way, Obama invited others to see themselves in her stories and to feel personally connected to her. The formulation of a positive, clearly defined persona that accentuated her understanding of others helped Obama become a respected and highly regarded first lady.

Melania Trump, who never had to be overly concerned with the tenor or depth of her public image, failed to effectively create a substantial persona that made her distinct from her husband in the 2016 campaign or in her first couple of years as the first lady. Instead, she simply stood next to or behind Donald at key moments and relied heavily on a media liaison to make most of her public statements. It was rare for Trump to share personal stories in public venues or to link her experiences to those of others. Even when she visited the detention centers for child immigrants separated from their families at the border, she did not try to show compassion and empathy by relying on her status as either a mother or as an immigrant. Instead, she participated in assorted photo opportunities (posing with children and with the officials running the centers).

One more unfair aspect of the comparisons between Michelle Obama and Melania Trump is the routine failure to account for the contextual elements of each woman's first ladyship. First ladies, while consequential and important, are not the central figure of a political campaign or the presidential administration in which they serve. Therefore, they are not entirely in control of their public image and activity. Public perceptions of the men they married, the tone and content of the messaging from their husbands, and the political era all impact the ways presidential spouses are interpreted and evaluated. In the cases of Michelle Obama and Melania Trump, understanding the circumstances of their move into the White House helps remind us of the unique challenges they confronted.

The 2008 Obama campaign mantra was an inclusive call for hope and change. The messaging surrounding the eventual president and his wife focused on shared American values, giving all citizens access to the American Dream, and transcending America's racially divisive past. The 2008 race was not free from negative elements and all candidates acknowledged there were problems to overcome, but the spirit of the eventual victor's campaign was mostly positive and had a broad-based appeal. Michelle Obama actively embraced the affirmative message. However, she did not simply parrot the words of her husband but built her own identity that incorporated the ideas of hope and change in a manner that related to her experiences as a wife and mother. Obama created an outward image that complemented and supported her husband, but that also allowed her to be an individual with her own perspectives and appeal.

The overarching themes of the 2016 Trump campaign were expressing anger and encouraging isolationism. From the very start, the candidate and his surrogates used insults and abusive rhetoric to gain attention and build a base of support among individuals with tendencies toward racism, sexism, and homophobia. As Donald Trump gained status in the party, his appeal widened, but he continued to claim he was giving voice to a purportedly oppressed majority that was tired of being forced into what he pejoratively called political correctness. The candidate and later president condoned violence against the press and against those who opposed his perspectives. Throughout the campaign, Melania Trump typically said little and did nothing to separate herself from her husband and his seemingly negative perspective. From the start, Michelle Obama had and took the opportunity to develop a positive and alluring persona. Melania Trump, meanwhile, started out shackled to a controversial figure and a contentious worldview.

The public portrayals of the relationships the women had with their husbands also influenced the way they were viewed as first lady. Michelle was usually depicted as an equal partner with Barack, whereas Melania was presented as the more quiet and deferential of the Trump pair. Michelle Obama openly talked about her disagreements with Barack, presumably made her own choices about her life, and negotiated with her husband when their interests conflicted. On the other hand, even before entering the White House, Melania Trump rarely contradicted Donald in public and often capitulated to him and his schemes even when she opposed them. Both women ultimately yielded to their husbands when it came to running for the presidency, but most descriptions of their decisions made it clear that Michelle Obama had genuine, regular, and meaningful input and Melania Trump did not.

Michelle Obama was rarely viewed as a compliant spouse even though she was very supportive of her husband and his political agenda. Obama did not openly challenge her husband on political matters, but she did complain about him on a personal level. She told stories about their home life that included harmless gripes that made him seem human and made her come across as relatable. She expressed frustrations about his diet and his smoking habit, tying them to her efforts to get people to make healthier life choices. Although her stated grievances were rather minor, her willingness to express them at all highlighted the fact that she did have her own perspectives that did not always align with her husband's point of view. In addition, Obama got her husband to support her initiatives as first lady. He made adjustments to his diet and exercise routine and made an effort to stop smoking in deference to her public platform. He also participated in social media messaging that encouraged physical activity and healthy decision-making. Her husband's cooperation signaled the camaraderie they shared and underscored the respect he had for her and her efforts.

After entering the White House, Melania Trump mostly retained her standing as an outwardly docile wife. Even as she showed some bits of her own personality, her actions never substantively challenged her husband in either a serious or humorous fashion. The statement she released on the separation of immigrant families at the border did not directly question her husband's policy but vaguely encouraged bipartisan legislative action. When she appeared to show support for someone her husband had attacked on Twitter, the first lady quickly backtracked and insisted she was not taking sides. Despite repeatedly expressing her concerns about cyberbullying, Trump refused to comment on her husband's social media tirades and his online harassment of a long list of individuals and groups. Melania Trump continued to come across as a subservient spouse once she assumed the mantle of the first lady, frustrating many people who wanted the White House matron to show some independence and personality.

Another part of the context that exacerbated Melania Trump's difficulty establishing a positive rapport with the public is that she followed a popular and competent first lady. The somewhat guarded and aloof Trump was such a dramatic change from the outgoing and candid Michelle Obama that complaints about Trump were inevitable. Without properly accounting for the variations in the women's skill sets and experiences as well as their preparation for life as a public servant and the contexts surrounding their assumption of the first ladyship, it might be reasonable to condemn Trump for being less accessible and effective than Obama. However, recognizing the limitations Trump had as she became the matron of the White House encourages a slightly more sympathetic reading of her efforts.

Michelle Obama and Melania Trump are two distinct women, with some notable similarities as well as a number of telling differences, who had to negotiate the undefined and amorphous duties that come along with being the first lady of the United States. The women had to manage life as a public person and a public servant because of their husbands' political ambitions. Like all of their forerunners, they had to adapt to the position while trying to find ways to make the post their own. The highly visible nature of the role meant they both also endured constant scrutiny.

Although it is understandable to try to categorize presidential spouses by type (e.g., traditional, modern, active, reserved, southern, etc.) and to compare various first ladies to those who preceded them, it is necessary to keep in mind that the job is problematic in many respects and that directly contrasting these women is fraught with challenges. The people who have filled the role have been real women with different experiences and unique worldviews who were confronting a variety of ever-changing, yet often amorphous, expectations. We should endeavor to understand Michelle Obama and Melania Trump as complex, multifaceted women rather than accepting the often-oversimplified caricatures offered of them by the press, online commentators, and those who would use them as political pawns. When assessing the various women who have overseen the East Wing of the White House, including Obama and Trump, it is important to remember that the first lady is "an unpaid public servant elected by one person, her husband."[2]

Notes

INTRODUCTION

1. Evgenia Peretz, "Inside the Trump Marriage: Melania's Burden," *Vanity Fair*, April 21, 2017, accessed May 6, 2018, https://www.vanityfair.com/news /2017/04/donald-melania-trump-marriage.

2. Andrea Park, "Inside the Small Slovenian Town Where Melania Trump Grew Up Under the Communist Regime," *People.com*, February 25, 2016, accessed April 13, 2018, http://people.com/politics/melania-trumps-childhood-in -communist-slovenia-in-poverty/.

1. AUDITIONING FOR FIRST LADY

1. Karrin Vasby Anderson, "The First Lady: A Site of 'American Woman- hood,'" in *Leading Ladies of the White House: Communication Strategies of Notable Twentieth-Century First Ladies*, ed. Molly Meijer Wertheimer (Lanham, MD: Rowman & Littlefield, 2005), 3.

2. David Bernstein, "The Speech," *Chicago Magazine*, May 29, 2007, accessed April 1, 2018, http://www.chicagomag.com/Chicago-Magazine/June-2007/The -Speech/.

3. Toby Harden, "Obama's Wife: His Secret Weapon," *The Age*, February 10, 2007, accessed April 1, 2018, https://www.theage.com.au/news/world/obamas -secret-weapon/2007/02/09/1170524298616.html.

4. Michelle Obama, "First Time Proud of USA," YouTube video, February 28, 2008, accessed May 26, 2018, https://www.youtube.com/watch?reload =9&v=LYY73RO_egw.

5. "Michelle Obama's America: Is Barack Obama's Wife His Rock or His Bitter Half?" *Economist*, July 3, 2008, accessed June 24, 2017, http://www.economist.com/node/11670246.

6. Maureen Dowd, "She's Not Buttering Him Up," *New York Times*, April 25, 2007, accessed April 1, 2018, https://www.nytimes.com/2007/04/25/opinion/25dowd.html.

7. Christi Parsons, Bruce Japsen, and Bob Secter, "Barack's Rock: Michelle Obama," *Chicago Tribune*, April 22, 2007, accessed April 1, 2018, http://www.chicagotribune.com/chi-070422michelle-story-archive-story.html.

8. Lydia Saad, "Melania Trump's Image Less Positive than Other Spouses," *Gallup.com*, July 18, 2016, accessed May 26, 2018, http://news.gallup.com/opinion/polling-matters/193793/melania-trump-image-problem-democrats-independents.aspx.

9. Saad, "Melania Trump's Image."

10. Tammy R. Vigil, "National Conventions: Evolving Functions and Forms," in *Political Campaign Communication: Theory, Method, and Practice*, ed. Robert E. Denton Jr. (Lanham, MD: Lexington Books, 2017).

11. Tammy R. Vigil, *Connecting with Constituents: Identification Building and Blocking in Contemporary National Convention Addresses* (Lanham, MD: Lexington Books, 2015).

12. Michelle Obama, "Transcript: Michelle Obama's 'One Nation,'" CNN, August 25, 2008, accessed June 30, 2013, http://www.cnn.com/2008/POLITICS/08/25/michelle.obama.transcript/.

13. Obama, "Transcript."

14. Will Drubhold, "Watch Melania Trump's Speech at the Republican Convention," *Time*, July 18, 2016, accessed August 1, 2016, http://time.com/4412008/republican-convention-melania-trump-2/.

15. Drubhold, "Watch Melania Trump's Speech."

16. "US Election: Full Transcript of Donald Trump's Obscene Videotape," BBC.com, October 9, 2016, accessed June 4, 2018, http://www.bbc.com/news/election-us-2016-37595321.

17. Laurel Elder, Brian Frederick, and Barbara Burrell, *American Presidential Candidate Spouses: The Public's Perspective* (New York: Palgrave Macmillan, 2018), 114.

2. THE TRANSITION TO THE WHITE HOUSE

1. Marc Schultz, "Obama Victory Speech, 2008," YouTube video, October 19, 2012, accessed June 7, 2018, https://www.youtube.com/watch?v=CnvUUauFJ98.

2. Ruth La Ferla, "That Dress? Everyone Has an Opinion," *New York Times*, November 5, 2008, accessed June 7, 2018, https://thecaucus.blogs.nytimes.com /2008/11/05/that-dress-everyone-has-an-opinion/.

3. Michelle Nichols, "Michelle Obama's Election Outfit Gets Dressing Down," Reuters, November 7, 2008, accessed June 7, 2018, https://www.reuters .com/article/us-usa-election-fashion/michelle-obamas-election-outfit-gets -dressing-down-idUSTRE4A65XA20081107.

4. Germaine Greer, "If Michelle Obama Is Such a Great Dresser, What Is She Doing in This Red Butcher's Apron?" *Guardian*, November 16, 2008, accessed June 7, 2018, https://www.theguardian.com/world/2008/nov/17 /michelleobama-fashion.

5. Nichols, "Michelle Obama's Election Outfit."

6. Kate Anderson Brower, "When First Ladies Meet: An Awkward Post-Election White House Tradition," *Washington Post*, April 6, 2016, accessed June 12, 2018, https://www.washingtonpost.com/lifestyle/style/when-first-ladies -meet-an-awkward-post-election-white-house-tradition/2016/04/06/5d8a60be -f6b6-11e5-9804-537defcc3cf6_story.html?utm_term=.3ab6c14f5cbf.

7. Krissah Thompson, "Melania Trump and Michelle Obama Carry on an Awkward Tradition, Too," *Washington Post*, November 10, 2016, accessed June 12, 2018, https://www.washingtonpost.com/lifestyle/style/melania-trump-and -michelle-obama-had-an-awkward-first-meeting-too/2016/11/10/2971efc6-a756 -11e6-ba59-a7d93165c6d4_story.html?utm_term=.45af53b9bbe5.

8. Brower, "When First Ladies Meet."

9. Leslie Bennetts, "Welcome to the White House, Mrs. Obama!" *Vanity Fair*, November 4, 2008, accessed June 8, 2018, https://www.vanityfair.com /news/2008/11/welcome-to-the-white-house-mrs-obama.

10. Michel Martin, "What Michelle Obama Is Giving Up," NPR, November 17, 2008, accessed June 8, 2018, https://www.npr.org/templates/story/story.php ?storyId=97082447.

11. Laurie Penny, "We Should Be Kind to America's First Victim—Melania Trump," *New Statesman*, December 15, 2016, accessed June 8, 2018, https://www .newstatesman.com/politics/feminism/2016/12/we-should-be-kind-americas -first-victim-melania-trump.

12. Joyce Walder, "A Model as First Lady? Think Traditional," *New York Times*, December 1, 1999, accessed July 11, 2018, https://www.nytimes.com/1999 /12/01/ nyregion/public-lives-a-model-as-first-lady-think-traditional.html.

13. Ana Veciana-Suarez, "The First Granny Has Left the White House, Too, and I'll Miss Her," *Miami Herald*, January 20, 2017, accessed June 9, 2018, http:// www.miamiherald.com/living/liv-columns-blogs/ana-veciana-suarez/article 127730439.html.

14. Kate Andersen Brower, "Ivanka Trump Could Be the Most Powerful First Lady Ever," *Washington Post*, December 16, 2016, accessed June 10, 2018, https://www.washingtonpost.com/posteverything/wp/2016/12/16/ivanka-trump-could-be-the-most-powerful-first-lady-ever/?noredirect=on&utm_term=.77c080547327.

15. Ruth Sherlock, "Melania Trump 'Won't Move into White House' as First Lady," *Telegraph*, November 20, 2016, accessed June 10, 2018, https://www.telegraph.co.uk/news/2016/11/20/melania-trump-wont-move-into-white-house-as-first-lady/.

16. Marjon Carlos, "Michelle Obama Leaves the White House in Classic Style," *Vogue*, January 20, 2017, accessed June 15, 2018, https://www.vogue.com/article/michelle-obama-barack-obama-inauguration.

17. Rachel Lubitz, "Michelle Obama's Inaugural Day Outfit: Outgoing FLOTUS Stuns (as Usual) in Red," *Mic*, January 20, 2017, accessed June 15, 2018, https://mic.com/articles/165988/michelle-obamas-inauguration-day-outfit-outgoing-flotus-stuns-as-usual-in-red#.KdgLCOSn1.

18. Sarah Wasilak, "This Might Be the Most Powerful Red Dress Michelle Obama's Ever Worn," *Pop Sugar*, January 29, 2017, accessed June 15, 2018, https://www.popsugar.com/fashion/Michelle-Obama-Red-Dress-Inauguration-2017-43028369.

19. Theresa Massony, "Donald Trump and Melania Awkwardly Dance at Inaugural Ball," *Elite Daily*, January 21, 2017, accessed June 17, 2018, https://www.elitedaily.com/news/politics/donald-trump-melania-first-dance-awkward/1761406.

3. FORGING THEIR OWN PATHS

1. Betty C. Monkman, "The White House State Dinner," White House Historical Association, accessed June 23, 2018, https://www.whitehousehistory.org/the-white-house-state-dinner.

2. Robin Gavhan and Roxanne Roberts, "Marking First State Dinner, Obama Welcomes Indian Prime Minister," *Washington Post*, November 25, 2009, accessed June 23, 2018, http://www.washingtonpost.com/wp-dyn/content/article/2009/11/24/AR2009112403529.html.

3. Kate Bennett, "Melania Trump Looks to History for Inspired State Dinner with the Macrons," CNN, April 23, 2018, accessed June 25, 2018, https://www.cnn.com/2018/04/21/politics/melania-trump-state-dinner/index.html.

4. Jenni Avins, "Melania Trump's State Dinner Gown Was Reincarnated from Chanel Couture Jumpsuit," Quartzy, April 24, 2018, accessed June 25, 2018, https://quartzy.qz.com/1261372/what-did-melania-trump-wear-to-the-state-dinner-chanel-couture/.

5. Michelle Obama, "Transcript: Michelle Obama's 'One Nation,'" CNN, August 25, 2008, accessed June 30, 2013, http://www.cnn.com/2008/POLITICS /08/25/michelle.obama.transcript/.

6. Elizabeth J. Natalle, "Michelle Obama's Ethos and *Let's Move!*" in *Michelle Obama: First Lady, American Rhetor*, ed. Elizabeth J. Natalle and Jenni M. Simon (Lanham, MD: Lexington Books, 2015), 70.

7. "Be Best," WhiteHouse.gov, accessed July 28, 2018, https://www .whitehouse.gov/bebest/.

8. Stephen Colbert, "Melania to Today's Youth: Be Best," *Late Show with Stephen Colbert*, May 7, 2018, accessed June 28, 2018, https://www.cbs.com/shows /the-late-show-with-stephen-colbert/video/14dFn19pWMYP0HI7eeK54a4fIK BIIi3d/melania-to-today-s-youth-be-best-/.

9. "First Lady Melania Trump Tweets 'Pray for Las Vegas,'" NBC News, October 2, 2017, accessed July 1, 2018, https://www.nbcnews.com/card/first-lady -melania-trump-tweets-pray-las-vegas-n806606.

4. CAN'T PLEASE EVERYONE

1. Kate Taylor, "The Cost Difference Between Melania Trump's and Michelle Obama's Outfits Reveals the Truth about America's Criticisms of Them," *Business Insider*, September 1, 2017, accessed July 22, 2018, http://www.business insider.com/first-lady-melania-trump-vs-michelle-obama-fashion-cost-of -clothing-2017-8.

2. Meghan Keneally, "Michelle Obama Says Husband Barack Has 'Swag' and Reveals She Regrets Wearing Shorts on Air Force One," *Daily Mail*, November 30, 2013, accessed July 22, 2018, http://www.dailymail.co.uk/news /article-2510569/Michelle-Obama-says-Air-Force-One-shorts-biggest-fashion -faux-pas.html.

3. Brian Trachman, "Alex Jones: 'Michelle Obama Is a Man' Who Murdered Joan Rivers to Cover It Up," *Right Wing Watch*, May 17, 2016, accessed July 23, 2018, http://www.rightwingwatch.org/post/alex-jones-michelle-obama-is-a -man-who-murdered-joan-rivers-to-cover-it-up/.

4. Claire Landsbaum, "West Virginia Mayor Resigns after She and Another Official Called Michelle Obama an 'Ape in Heels' in Facebook Post," *The Cut*, November 15, 2016, accessed July 23, 2018, https://www.thecut.com/2016/11 /west-virginia-officials-called-michelle-obama-ape-in-heels.html.

5. Sarah A. Harvard, "Georgia Teacher Jane Wood Allen Fired over Racist Facebook Posts about Michelle Obama," *Mic*, October 4, 2016, accessed July 23, 2018, https://mic.com/articles/155796/georgia-teacher-jane-wood-allen-fired -over-racist-facebook-posts-about-michelle-obama#.ce1xkARMy.

6. Ed Mazza, "Mayor Calls Barack Obama 'Monkey Man,' and Michelle Obama 'Gorilla Face,' but Says He's Not Racist," *Huffington Post*, July 16, 2015, accessed July 23, 2018, https://www.huffingtonpost.com/entry/washington -mayor-racist_us_55a71677e4b04740a3defd84.

7. Claire Zillman, "The Subtle Power of Melania Trump's Poker Face," *Fortune*, May 25, 2017, accessed July 23, 2018, http://fortune.com/2017/05/25 /melania-trump-smile-overseas-trip/.

8. Scott Clement, "The Most Popular Obama Wasn't the President," *Washington Post*, December 12, 2016, accessed July 24, 2018, https://www.washington post.com/graphics/national/obama-legacy/michelle-obama-popularity.html.

9. Jonathan P. Hicks, "Commentary: Insulting Michelle Obama Seems to Be the New Sport of the Right," BET, January 9, 2012, accessed July 14, 2017, http://www.bet.com/news/national/2012/01/09/commentary-insulting -michelle-obama-seems-to-be-the-new-sport-of-the-right.html.

10. Alix Langone, "All Five Living First Ladies Speak Out against Border Family Separation Policy," *Time*, June 19, 2018, accessed July 27, 2018, http:// time.com/5315482/first-ladies-trumps-border-family-separation-policy/.

11. Laura Bush, "Separating Children from Their Parents at the Border 'Breaks My Heart,'" *Washington Post*, June 17, 2018, accessed July 27, 2018, https://www.washingtonpost.com/opinions/laura-bush-separating-children -from-their-parents-at-the-border-breaks-my-heart/2018/06/17/f2df517a-7287 -11e8-9780-b1dd6a09b549_story.html?utm_term=.4790fca7c064.

12. Langone, "All Five Living First Ladies Speak Out."

13. Kate Bennett, "Melania Trump 'Hates to See' Children Separated from Their Families at Borders," CNN, June 18, 2018, accessed July 27, 2018, https:// www.cnn.com/2018/06/17/politics/melania-trump-children-separated -immigration/index.html.

5. PRESIDENTIAL ELECTION, ROUND TWO

1. Eleanor Sheehan, "People Freaked Out Over This Comment Hillary Clinton Made in 1992," PopSugar, August 19, 2016, accessed August 1, 2018, https:// www.popsugar.com/news/Hillary-Clinton-Baking-Cookies-Comment -42252587.

2. Terence Hunt, "The Day Outspoken Barbara Bush Regretted Speaking Her Mind," *Boston Globe*, April 28, 2018, accessed August 5, 2018, https://www .boston.com/news/politics/2018/04/18/the-day-outspoken-barbara-bush -regretted-speaking-her-mind.

3. Nancy Gibbs, "Remembering Nancy Reagan: The End of a White House Love Story," *Time*, March 6, 2016, accessed August 5, 2018, http://time.com /4248899/nancy-reagan-death-obituary/.

4. Maureen Dowd, "I Read, I Smoke, I Spin," *New York Times*, February 22, 2004, accessed June 4, 2017, http://www.nytimes.com/2004/02/22/opinion /i-read-i-smoke-i-spin.html?_r=0.

AFTERWORD

1. Carl Brown, "Then and Now: First Ladies," *Roper Center for Public Opinion Research*, accessed August 8, 2018, https://ropercenter.cornell.edu/then-and -now-first-ladies/.

2. Quote attributed to Lady Bird Johnson. See Scarlet Neath, "What's the Point of a First Lady?" *Atlantic*, October 6, 2015, accessed August 10, 2018, https://www.theatlantic.com/politics/archive/2014/10/whats-the-point-of-a -first-lady/380753/.

Selected Bibliography

Blair, Diane M. "No Ordinary Time: Eleanor Roosevelt's Address to the 1940 Democratic National Convention." *Rhetoric & Public Affairs* 4 (2001): 203–222. https://doi.org/10.1353/rap.2001.0021.

Borelli, MaryAnne. *The Politics of the President's Wife*. College Station: Texas A&M University Press, 2011.

Burrell, Barbara, Laurel Elder, and Brian Frederick. "From Hillary to Michelle: Public Opinion and the Spouses of Presidential Candidates." *Presidential Studies Quarterly* 41 (2011): 156–176. https://doi.org/10.1111/j.1741-5705.2010.03835.x.

Campbell, Karlyn Khors. "The Rhetorical Presidency: A Two-Person Career." In *Beyond the Rhetorical Presidency*, edited by Martin J. Medhurst, 179–198. College Station: Texas A&M University Press, 1996.

Carlin, Diana, and Nancy Kegan Smith. "First Lady Michelle Obama: The American Dream Endures, II." In *A Companion to First Ladies*, edited by Katherine A. S. Sibley, 696–715. Malden, MA: Wiley-Blackwell, 2016.

Caroli, Betty Boyd. *First Ladies: From Martha Washington to Michelle Obama*. New York: Oxford University Press, 2010.

Elder, Laurel, Brian Frederick, and Barbara Burrell. *American Presidential Candidate Spouses: The Public's Perspective*. New York: Palgrave Macmillan, 2018.

Gutin, Myra G. *The President's Partner: The First Lady in the Twentieth Century*. Westport, CT: Praeger, 1989.

Hummer, Jill Abraham. *First Ladies and American Women: In Politics and at Home*. Lawrence, KS: University Press of Kansas, 2017.

Knuckey, Jonathan, and Myunghee Kim. "Evaluations of Michelle Obama as First Lady: The Role of Racial Resentment." *Presidential Studies Quarterly* 46 (2016): 365–386. https://doi.org/10.1111/psq.12274.

Mandziuk, Roseann M. "Whither the Good Wife? 2016 Presidential Candidate Spouses in the Gendered Spaces of Contemporary Politics." *Quarterly Journal of Speech* 103 (2017): 136–159. https://doi.org/10.1080/00335630.2016.1233350.

Natalle, Elizabeth J., and Jenni M. Simon, eds. *Michelle Obama: First Lady, American Rhetor.* Lanham, MD: Lexington Books, 2015.

O'Conner, Karen, Bernadette Nye, and Laura Van Assendelft. "Wives in the White House: The Political Influence of First Ladies." *Presidential Studies Quarterly* 26 (1996): 835–853. http://jstor.org/stable/27551636.

Parry-Giles, Shawn J. *Hillary Clinton in the News: Gender and Authenticity in American Politics.* Chicago: University of Illinois Press, 2014.

Parry-Giles, Shawn J., and Diane M. Blair. "The Rise of the Rhetorical First Lady: Politics, Gender Ideology, and Women's Voice, 1789–2002." *Rhetoric & Public Affairs* 4, no. 4 (2002): 565–600. https://doi.org/10.1353/rap.2003.0011.

Smith, Nancy Kegan, and Diana Carlin. "First Lady Michelle Obama: The American Dream Endures, I." In *A Companion to First Ladies*, edited by Katherine A. S. Sibley, 677–695. Malden, MA: Wiley-Blackwell, 2016.

Vigil, Tammy R. "Feminine Views in the Feminine Style: Convention Speeches by Presidential Nominees' Spouses." *Southern Communication Journal* 79, no. 4 (2014): 327–346. https://doi.org/10.1080/1041794X.2014.916339.

Wertheimer, Molly Meijer, ed. *Leading Ladies of the White House: Communication Strategies of Notable Twentieth-Century First Ladies.* Lanham, MD: Rowman & Littlefield, 2005.

Index

Page numbers in *italics* refer to figures.

TAMMY R. VIGIL, PhD, is Associate Professor of Communication at Boston University. She studies political campaign rhetoric and women as political communicators. Dr. Vigil's recent books include *Moms in Chief: The Rhetoric of Republican Motherhood and the Spouses of Presidential Nominees, 1992–2016* and *Connecting with Constituents: Identification Building and Blocking in Contemporary National Convention Addresses*. She has also published journal articles and book chapters on rhetoric by Michelle Obama, Franklin D. Roosevelt, and George W. Bush; on the history of nominating conventions; and on convention speeches by presidential nominees' spouses. Dr. Vigil formerly served as Associate Dean of the College of Communication at Boston University and is a past winner of the Wrange-Baskerville Award given by the Public Address Division of the National Communication Association.

ACQUISITIONS EDITOR   Ashley Runyon

PROJECT MANAGER   Darja Malcolm-Clarke

BOOK & COVER DESIGN   Pam Rude

COMPOSITION   Tony Brewer